Front Cover Photograph:
Inside the largest factory building designed in 1920's by Thomas
Falconer, Stroud Architect well known for his Arts and Crafts
designs.
A view of the site in 1951 after the new office block was completed.

Rear cover photograph:
Family members and office staff in 1942 celebrate 50 years of
Frederick Daniels' service to the company.

1

Daniels of Stroud

The history of a family engineering firm.

Chris Daniels

T.H. & J Daniels 1951

Copies of this book are available from www.danielsofstroud.co.uk, and from most high street bookshops.
chris@danielsofstroud.co.uk

First published 2018

ISBN 9781999640705

Copyright Chris Daniels 2018

Published by Daniels
15 Victoria Road,
Retford. Notts
DN22 7DJ
www.danielsofstroud.co.uk

For Daniels past & present;

family, friends, staff and workers.

Preface

I am a Daniels, and in the beginning I was interested in the stories told to me of the great Daniels dynasty and how it came about. My fascination with historic research was fuelled because, despite living and working in a time where everything happens in an instant, research cannot be hurried. I started years ago, pre-internet, when you had to make personal visits to the bowels of St Catherine's House in London and pore through original documents; later it transferred to the Family Record Centre – that's gone now. A lot of information is now on the internet, although I include research from Kew Records Office, the British Library, the Church of the Latter Day Saints & Mormon Archives, the family Bible, the British Newspaper Library, local Records Offices, the Alfred Herbert Museum, churchyards, various books and, of course, the family. I feel privileged to have handled some of the original documents, and somehow it seems less 'real' on the internet.

I have been fortunate that the buildings on the manufacturing site remain intact, as if in a time capsule, and that the Daniels photographically recorded everything manufactured, creating probably the best record of manufacturing development from 1890 to 1970 of any business in the country: over 4000 photographs. This I believe to be unique.

This book is a summary of the research I have carried out. It is not complete; it may never be! It is being produced at a time when the future of the manufacturing site is uncertain. The development of the company can be seen through its building which form an important part of the history of the business and have remained relatively intact; however plans are in place for them to be demolished.

The Stroud area played an important part in industrial development in the second industrial revolution, in many ways it 'hit above its weight' in technical matters. Most manufacturing sites in the country from the period are associated with a single industry or product, they made cloth, developed motorcycles or parts for trains, but Daniels were involved in every industry and were behind the success of businesses in the valley's, they were pioneers in engineering and production, they were the power house to industry, developing machines to carry out traditional tasks, working on new products, designing equipment for mass-production lines, working with the latest materials, pioneering plastics and rubber, expert metallurgists and chemical engineers, world leading inventors with a raft of patented 'ideas'. They were a company of global significance and the importance of the site and the records to industrial archaeology cannot be overstressed.

With the growth in tourism and the tourist sector accounting for a significant portion of UK Gross Domestic Product, there is a major argument to utilise our industrial heritage sites; and for Stroud, Daniels is central and of such importance that, in my opinion, it is of 'World Heritage' significance and could be developed in a similar vein as Magna in Rotherham, The Ironbridge Gorge or The Big Pit in South Wales.

I consider myself an amateur in historical research: my career has been in engineering. I apologise to all those experts who have carried out a lifetime in research, and find unorthodox methodology, but I believe a background in engineering has helped in the research. My aim has been to record some of the stories from the family and combine it with the facts as recorded in the public domain and in private hands. Material is reproduced with the intention of illustrating the story, and any proceeds from book sales will be used for research. In parts I have used 'artistic licence' to try to paint a picture of how our history evolved and some of the events and technological advances that impacted on it. I accept this may not meet convention and may not always be correct, but it records my voyage of discovery. I apologise in advance if I may have missed the point or misread some of the documentation (some early records are barely legible!); please let me know if there are errors that you know about, or indeed have memories of your own that are connected to the story. I found some of the memories sad; I'm sure others will too, and whilst I do not wish to 'rake though old ground', I feel the story needs telling. Some of the events within living memory may be remembered differently by others, I have tried to use records to corroborate the information told to me.

During the course of my research I met a gentleman who had been an apprentice to Daniels some forty years earlier. When I explained I was a Daniels he willingly recounted his story, and I was particularly moved when he praised Daniels for such an excellent apprenticeship that had seen him through his career; 'a Daniels apprenticeship opened doors, and it was such a great company to work for' – he recounted that he had a lot of fun. I was reminded of the speech passed on to me that was given by John Daniels (Senior) at the company's centenary, of which copies exist, that praised the workers, acknowledging that it was their skill and dedication that was at the heart of the business. It served to confirm my findings that

6

there was considerable affection through the company, that the Daniels' were great leaders and had a great workforce. This book is dedicated in part to all those people who worked to make Daniels the company it was and who, in turn, played their part in the making, and saving of a Great Britain.

I also dedicate this edition to my family: my parents Peter & Dorothy, who have helped me with their memories and support, and my wife Louise and children, Rebecca & Edward, who have been patient when other jobs I should have been doing have been left undone.

Biography

Continuing with the family tradition in Engineering, Christopher graduated with a B.Sc. in Electrical Engineering from Salford University in 1984. He worked at Telemetrix, where the company designed and manufactured some of the first computers specifically for drawing offices. He was involved in most aspects of a business that was growing fast and floated on the Stock Exchange. He ran several special projects and was also fortunate to travel to the Far East and the US, seeing other companies involved in the early electronics industry.

In 1991 he moved to join STC, which was taken over to become Northern Telecom and later Alcatel. He was at their Greenwich site manufacturing Sub-Sea Cable Systems for global telecommunications, where he was involved in the first optically amplified Fibre Optic Cable Networks and worked on high reliability product designs, rising to the position of Development Manager.

In 1998 he left to assume the position of Technical Manager at COE PLC, manufacturing CCTV products and systems, where he was responsible for all aspects of design and development. In addition, he ran several major manufacturing projects, including the CCTV network for the London Charging Scheme.

He left COE to set up a website design agency and currently runs this alongside The Big Country House Ltd, a holiday home business providing country house holidays to groups in Nottinghamshire. Most recently he set up and is Director of the North Notts Artisan and Tourist Information Centre CIC, a tourist centre with an art gallery and artisan craft centre, farm shop, café, artisan studios and Pilgrim Fathers Museum in Retford, North Nottinghamshire.

Introduction

The Daniels family of Stroud are still remembered today for their great engineering business of the early 20th century, T.H. & J. Daniels, and by others in the area for their involvement with many aspects of the community; but the extraordinary story is one of intense activity within the fast-developing industrial framework of Britain and of a family who worked their way out of poverty, moving up the social scale.

This is the story of an industrious family, which looks at their history to find out what they were like, and investigates the social, industrial and political influences that enabled the meteoric rise of their industrial business. In doing so, it discovers the story of a family who were extraordinarily dynamic and whose reach included rule in Victorian India, early clocks, Napoleon Bonaparte, manufacture of the first teddy bears, patents & inventions, the Masonic Order, Mormons and the early Scout movements. At the heart of this rags-to-riches story was a blacksmith's business that was touched by the Industrial Revolution to become one of the biggest family-owned engineering businesses in the region.

The Daniels created a photographic record of the machines and products made on their manufacturing site – in total around 4000 photographs, everything from Bridges, Cable Cars, Stoves, Pin Machines, Walking Stick machines, Engines, Turbines to Ammunitions, Rocket Launchers and Tanks. It shows how they were involved in war activities as well as pivotal developments in world advances such as plastics, jet engine design and ballistics. It is a record of industrial development and technology from the later parts of the Victorian era through to the computer age, and demonstrates the development from bespoke manufacture to mass production. It shows how the development of new materials affected engineering and product development. It also shows how manufacturing sites developed to accommodate changes in technology.

9

Contents

Chapter 1.   Life before T.H. & J. Daniels

The name Daniels is purported to be of Welsh origin. South Wales is certainly an area synonymous with the science of metalworking, with its smelting furnaces and availability of coal and iron, and it may have been here that the family learned their skills. Wales also has the greatest number of Tabernacles, the place of faith for a non-conformist movement that continued to run through the veins of the Daniels family into the 20th century. However, there is no direct link to Wales and no evidence of Daniels metalworking skills prior to the 18th century.

Indeed, it is difficult to identify our ancestors from the church records that still exist. However, I believe that the earliest record pertinent to our family is a record showing a Giles Daniell born in 1591 in Warminster, Wiltshire. Giles moved to the village of Frampton-on-Severn in Gloucestershire, where he had a son called Giles. Giles (the second) married Tabitha and had a son, John, who moved to the next village of Westbury-on-Severn and married Elizabeth. They had a son Isaak or Isaac, who was born in 1698. Isaac married Anne Bird in 1726 in Minchinhampton, near Stroud, and had two sons, Richard, born the year after, and William, born 1733. From Richard we can make a link to Thomas who was father to another Thomas Daniels who started T.H. & J Daniels..

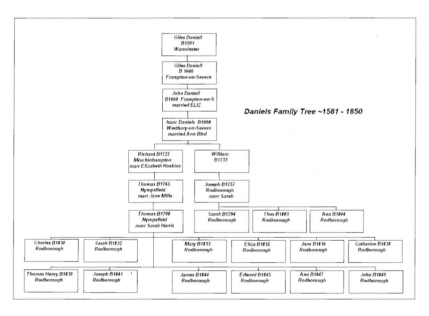

Daniels Family Tree ~1581 - 1850

Meanwhile, there are records of Daniels in Rodborough, but I cannot be certain where these relate to our family. The earliest record of the Daniels family in Rodborough was the birth of William in 1693 to Nathaniel. Then followed Thomas in

1687, Jonathan in 1695, Sarah in 1697 and David in 1700. Often families named offspring after other family members, and these are all names that appear later in our family history; however, I am unable to link these directly into the blood line. Was Nathaniel the son of John from Westbury-on-Severn? William of Rodborough had a son William in 1716. In 1727 John was born; he married Ann Davis. In 1757 Joseph was born to William, but we don't know whether this was Isaac's son or William of Rodborough's, who married Sarah and had Sarah (1794), Thomas (1803) and Ann (1804). If William was Isaac's son, then the family in Rodborough were related.

Richard of Minchinhampton moved to Nympsfield, married Elizabeth Hoskins and had a son, Thomas (senior), in 1765. Thomas (senior) married Jane Mills in 1786 and had a son, Thomas (junior), who was born in 1798 in Nympsfield. We know Thomas (junior) became a blacksmith and nailworker and Richard, his brother, was an ironworker. We also know Thomas (senior) was a blacksmith and there are records of John and William Daniels serving blacksmith apprenticeships in 1799 at Caleb Fords in Bagpath, a small hamlet just a few miles south of Nympsfield. Thomas's father died when he was a baby; the elder brothers will have taken over the blacksmithing business and as Thomas (junior) grew up he will have been looked after by the family. But Nympsfield was not big enough to support all the brothers, and some will have moved away to set up elsewhere.

Apprenticeship records

We don't know how Thomas ended up in Rodborough. It may be that he went to live with his uncle, or maybe a brother had set up a blacksmith's and so he went to serve an apprenticeship, or he had to move away from Nypsfield to find work, but by 1829 he was in Rodborough, where in 1829 he married Sarah Harris.

Baptism record for Thomas, son of Richard dated 1765.

This sets our story, with Thomas and Sarah married in Rodborough and setting up home at Church Place, a small square beside the church in the centre of the village.

12

Chapter 2. From Blacksmithing to the Lightpill Iron Works.

By the 19th century most villages would have had a blacksmith to provide metal-worked items, such as shoes for the horses to till the land, hinges, locks and basic ironwork for houses, knives and saws, ploughs, parts for carts and farming implements. In most villages the smithy would have been central to the village, located near the church, pub or village green. Most blacksmiths continued in existence catering for horses until the car in the early 20th century, then diversified to provide garages for fuel and service.

At some stage Thomas left Nympsfield and moved to Rodborough, possibly to another part of the Daniels family. Without his father to guide him, he will have served an apprenticeship and learned his trade, and maybe the family he lived with in Rodborough were also blacksmiths; it is unlikely that his family could have paid for his apprenticeship. The first records of him in operation as a blacksmith place him at Rose Cottage in Church Place in 1829. He was a nail-maker, a role that requires greater skill than a blacksmith because iron contained impurities that required hammering out, and most of the impurities needed removing for nails. The central village position will have been ideal for a blacksmith, and within reach of Stroud, where business was thriving.

Rose Cottage where Thomas lived, now known as Rose Villa. The original forge would have been the outbuilding on front of the property.

He will have had a workshop with a forge. His raw ingredient, pig iron, will have been bought in from a company that would have smelted iron ore to produce rough iron cylinders. These contained impurities, mostly carbon, that would be removed by heating and hammering as the required item was forged into shape. The pig iron, together with the coal, was carried to Stroud by barge on the canal.

In 1829, at the age of thirty-one, Thomas married Sarah Harris. Over the next few years they had many children: Charles, Sarah, Mary, Eliza, Jane, Catherine, Thomas, Joseph, James, Edward, Ann and John, all living in Church Place. Times were tough, and as soon as the children were able to help out, they did.

The blacksmith's was the start of the business that was to become T.H. & J. Daniels. Thomas started in 1829, but the date for the start of the business has always been known as 1840 and it was this date that was given at the centenary celebrations over a century later. We also know that he was in operation in 1835. This presents an anomaly. There is an additional problem with the size of the premises. The building at Rose Cottage is large enough for a small forge, but it is not big enough for the number of workers who, we believe, worked at the business before it transferred to a larger site on Bath Road in 1875. It is listed that there were sixteen employees in 1871. In addition, we know that the first foundry built on that new site was a brass foundry rather than an iron foundry and we would have expected an iron foundry to come first. However, there is an industrial site in Church Place, which is now a car repair garage. It may have been that it was here that the first iron foundry was constructed in 1840, and that this was seen as the start of the business.

The Garage in Church Place and map showing Rose Cottage with the Garage location at the top of the map.

It is interesting to note that by 1851 there was Cook's millwright next door, the two businesses able to offer complementary services of carpentry and metalworking skills to the public. Again, it is more likely that they were both on the industrial site. The business continued to grow in Church Place and eventually other workers were taken on to cope with demand.

Much of the work will have been repetitive: hinges, locks, gates and many other items which could be standardized through the introduction of an iron foundry. In addition, it enabled an expansion of the range of work that could be accommodated. Models of the various items were made from wood, then this was impressed in a black sand to create a mould called a patten.

A furnace called a puddling furnace was used to melt the pig iron, to which other ingredients were also added; that resulted in a purer iron that was then poured into the moulds.

An example of a typical foundry, located at Blists Hill, Shropshire.
Joseph Daniels's Birth Certificate

For our story, the two key sons were Thomas Henry, who was born in 1839 and Joseph, born on 5 Dec 1840.

As the boys grew up they were in an environment of industrial activity and will have worked in the business. James, Edward and John became involved in the carpentry, Thomas Henry and Joseph helped his father in the forge. The 1851 census records Sarah and Catherine as having left home and working as servants in Stroud for John Cox; Sarah was nineteen, Catherine was just thirteen. The 1861 census records Sarah as working as a nurse in service amongst other staff for a Prussian merchant at a big house in Surrey.

As the boys came of an age to do so, it is likely that they worked to serve apprenticeships. There was great demand for young lads to work alongside more skilled men, particularly in the railways, and eldest son Charles travelled to Reading and worked for a Mr John Smart as a blacksmith, together with Harry Dudfield, a lad three years older than Charles from Newent, John's sons not being old enough to help him themselves. By 1861 Charles was working in Paddington in Middlesex; he had married Maria and had children: Charles, Mary and Sarah, George and Francis.

Mary Daniels, born 1834, the eldest daughter, married John Shand Hutchings, a spring-maker in Paddington, London in 1863. It is possible she was introduced through Charles.

Thomas Henry continued working with his father, while James, Edward and John were probably apprenticed next door at Cook's. James went on to become a cabinetmaker and Edward and John became millwrights.

As time went on there was more income into the family and they had sufficient funds for a son to serve an apprenticeship in another company further afield; it was Joseph who had a natural talent, and so he went to London when he reached

15

sixteen to serve his apprenticeship at Hayward Taylor. It was an apprenticeship that he did not complete, because his father died.

Thomas Daniels

On 5 January 1863 Thomas died, forcing Joseph and Charles to return to Rodborough to help out in the busy family business. Thomas Henry was a natural businessman and very much in charge, so by 1871 Charles, who had his own career and was more accustomed to regular employment, found work in Chester as a foreman smith. By now Charles's eldest son, Charles, was also trained as a fitter and turner and also worked in Rodborough, until he returned to London and later became a Freeman of the City of London.

Thomas Daniels's headstone in Rodborough Church yard.

Most of the family continued to live together in Church Place with Thomas's wife, Sarah, now head of the household. Thomas Henry ran the business, ably assisted by Joseph, and it continued to grow. But the location in Church Place proved to be a constraint. The land around Church Place is steep and access via the small lanes

16

was difficult. The area was becoming quickly built up and limited any expansion plans that they might have had. Whether they owned the cottage and land is unknown, but it may have made sense to invest profits into their own premises, where they could construct workshops.

Sadly, in 1867, James, aged just twenty-three, died.

Joseph was thirty-two when he married Clara Ada Isacke in 1871. We can only assume the brothers to have been so busy with business – and indeed everything they had was put back into it to maintain its growth – that marriage was a low priority. Clara Ada Isacke was a well-educated scholar and school principal, daughter of a successful businessman manufacturing brushes, and part of an industrious family. Clara had two sisters and together they started a school in Stroud that they ran for many years, as we shall see later. Joseph Daniels, a successful engineer who was leading a thriving and growing family business, together with Clara, created a highly successful combination. It is possible that she had a dowry, a sum of money paid to Joseph for him to care for her, and that this helped with the next stage of the development of his business.

Photographs of Clara Ada: an early photo and a locket kept by John Stewart.

In 1873 Edward married Katherine, a local girl born in Rodborough, and they set up home at Sion House on the road to the Tabernacle. John was still single; he lodged with them and their ever-expanding family. As technology improved, both Edward and John made a natural progression from millwrights to engine fitters. Edward and Katherine moved to Inchbrook, where they had a son, John E, who went on to become an estate agent, and a son, Arthur, who became an engineer's iron fitter for a gas engine manufacturer, possibly for the Dudbridge Iron Works, which was nearby.

17

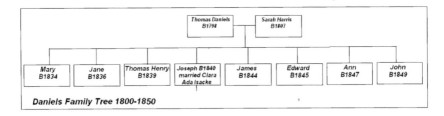

Thomas Daniels B1798		Sarah Harris B1807					
Mary B1834	Jane B1836	Thomas Henry B1839	Joseph B1840 married Clara Ada Isacke	James B1844	Edward B1845	Ann B1847	John B1849

Daniels Family Tree 1800-1850

In 1875, Thomas's wife Sarah died. She was buried with Thomas at St Mary Magdalene's Church opposite their cottage. The same year heralded many other changes that resulted in the formation of the Lightpill Iron Works and a new site on the main A46 route out of Stroud with good access to road, rail and canal.

They invested in treadle lathes for metal turning and used 'hand graving tools' to work designs by hand. In the 1860's and 70's they built several 'beam engines' and steam engines as they acquired new skills in design and manufacture. They were involved in Guttermuth high speed pumps from as early as this period before 1900. The business worked on 'still engines' that used both a piston driven by a steam boiler and a combustion engine simultaneously, a feat of engineering in those days! The company made the Hele Shaw Streamline filters that could be used for filtering liquids like oil or beer to remove impurities.

Advert for filters from 1930's and 1900 Daniels 'Valve Engine'

Chapter 3. Thomas Henry and the Umbrella Company

Thomas Henry was an entrepreneur, and in addition to the blacksmith's business he started to become involved in other ventures. He started a business making umbrella furniture with James Smith of Inchbrook and Richard Cook from Sheffield. We don't know exactly when it was started, but in 1874 the partnership was dissolved and Thomas took over the business. At some point he then went into co-partnership with Joseph and with Edward Bizzy Hooper, running the same business. The business, based at nearby Inchbrook, was called T.H. Daniels & Co. The business was put into receivership in December 1876 and all debts were paid by Edward.

A Daniels turning machine for zinc and brass umbrella notches and a later automatic machine for turning out zinc furniture, both from around 1880.

The Stroud valleys were one of the most important walking-stick and umbrella manufacturing areas in the world. Believed to have been started by William Dangerfield in the 1840's, the industry grew to employ thousands of people in over twenty large mills for the next hundred years. The Hooper family had been involved in walking stick manufacturing from an early period and owned Griffins Mill from 1856 to produce walking- and umbrella sticks. It was a natural progression for the Hoopers to have become involved in associated products. We don't know why the business failed, but the Hooper family later also invested in the T.H. & J. Daniels business.

The use of umbrellas by the public was both functional and highly fashionable in the late Victorian period. Initially hand-crafted, the advent of machines allowed the mechanical metal parts, called 'umbrella furniture' to be formed in increasing quantities for the mass markets. The quality of steel was insufficient to achieve the fine detail and so either brass or zinc was used to form the parts. Many patents for machines were filed both in the US and Great Britain between 1870 and 1890. Daniels produced a number of machines; earlier machines were based on lathes and later special automatic machines.

By 1889 the umbrella furniture business was trading as Marmont & Taylor. Joseph Marmont, together with Albert Perkings and Henry Critchley, had a pin-

19

making business at Frogmarsh Mill that was reasonably successful, although it was a very competitive industry. Pin-making was an important industry, and at this time the French had several large manufacturers, but in 1870, during the Prussian War, the Germans destroyed six major French pin-making companies. Critchley travelled to Paris and secured much of the business, which enabled their company to flourish.

Daniels also manufactured pin-making machines, and so for Marmont it will have been a reasonable progression to have produced umbrella furniture on the Daniels notching machines within his pin-making company.

Eventually, Marmont's son, Arthur, was of the age to become involved in the business, but the other partners refused until their sons were also old enough; as a result, Marmont invested in the Daniels family business and bought the walking-stick furniture business at Inchbrook for his son to run. He then went to London to work as an accountant. Eventually, his son did start at the pin-making company, which continued to make pins until 1936. The Marmont & Taylor business continued until sometime after 1919. The investment in Daniels helped to enable Joseph and Thomas Henry to buy a mill at Cam shortly after, as we shall see later.

Walking stick bending machine.

20

Chapter 4. Setting the Scene: the Stroud Valleys.

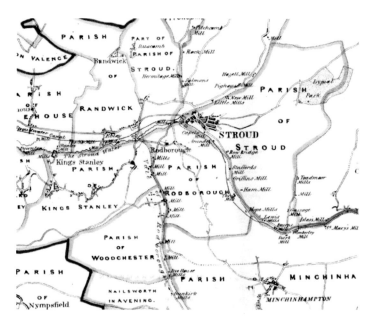

Dawson's map of Stroud 1830 showing mills in Rodborough Valley and a mill on the site chosen for Daniels. Note Nympsfield bottom left.

Stroud is a small town in Gloucestershire located at the convolution of five valleys. Equidistant between Birmingham and Bristol, with Gloucester as the nearest city, it was not a particularly important medieval settlement. By the 19th century it was a mill town and had been for two hundred years. Sheep grazed the hills and the valleys were littered with Cotswold stone mills to house the fleeces and the production of fine cloth.

The Stroudwater Canal was built between 1775 and 1779 to enable the transport of goods, primarily from the woollen mills to the customers in the cities and overseas to the rest of the empire via the Severn Estuary. The advent of the canal will have sealed the importance of the area and in time more woollen mills and other businesses developed.

But the area had few natural resources of its own, no iron or coal, and wood was limited because the upper reaches and steep valleys did not lend themselves to forestation. But the area did have an abundance of small streams, and water coursed down the valleys. The canal was key in the early development of the area

21

because it could be used for bringing in the resources that the area lacked: iron, coal and wood from the Forest of Dean, around twenty miles away.

The developments in the mills in the earlier parts of the Industrial Revolution required machinery for manufacture and water wheels to harness power from the streams. Stroud was not a pioneer in the earlier industrial period of the revolution in the 19th century, being too far from the prime industrial areas of the Black Country and the harbour at Bristol, although there were a few sparks of entrepreneurship.

But Stroud followed the nation's progress in mechanisation and developed cloth looms that in turn produced some fine cloth, a wide range and in large volumes, most famously baize used for billiard tables, and with a unique coloured dye. To make looms and machines, a fine carpentry industry developed, skilled people used to dealing with materials and having a good special awareness to see how things can be made to fit together.

But wooden parts wear and there are limitations in strength and size, and so a skilled blacksmith with a small foundry near the heart of Stroud will have provided the opportunity for some clever innovative ideas to be incorporated to improve production. This supported the manufacture of these machines for cloth production as well as machines designed for specific applications like stick manufacture or pin-making. In addition, demand for traditional products for carts for transport and horseshoes will have been high. Thus the business in the 19th century was in demand and flourished.

The first Stroud railway was opened in 1845, creating demand on three fronts: firstly, it required iron piece parts cast for its construction, including a number of bridges; secondly, it created new markets for the goods from the valleys and further mill development; and thirdly it opened up markets for products manufactured in the valleys in London and the other large cities. Later, the railway was brought to nearby Dudbridge in 1886 as a private venture by a number of local industrialists. This enabled larger, heavier items to be moved more easily: cast fireplaces, stoves and baths destined for the housing booms of the cities, and later large boilers, heavy girders and large machines for industrial use.

Chapter 5. Industrial Revolution

To help understand the progress of the Daniels family it is useful to understand the context of industrialisation in Great Britain as well as in the Stroud valleys.

The 1700's had seen the invention of machines with the infamous spinning jenny and the steam engine, but their application was limited and the impact of the technologies was not fully felt. The period from 1793 to 1815 was marked by the French Revolutionary Wars, which involved Great Britain to an extent and cost the country financially, leaving the Government with a debt of £850M by 1816. In addition, unemployment was high because the new spinning machines were putting many out of work, and farms were also undergoing dramatic mechanisation changes. To add to the problems, after the wars were finished, around 250,000 men returned home.

There followed a depression from 1816 to 1830. The 'laissez-faire' period where Government expected that the economy would recover despite the mass of legislation to the contrary. But it didn't.

The study of Economics was in its infancy; they did not know what the economic effects of Government policy would be and were worried that if they acted, they would make the situation worse and more of the working class would perish. However, ultimately they had no option as the situation continued to deteriorate and the 'Reformers' instigated change that eventually had a significant positive effect.

Of interest to us are, firstly, the changes to the Poor Law. Until 1825 if someone was unable to work they could receive a 'doles' payment from their parish, but they had to be in their parish to receive it. This stopped people moving to find work, a major disadvantage since many of the unemployed were in rural areas from farms and rural activities. It was replaced by workhouses, which were a less costly method of looking after the unemployed than 'doles' payments. Generally workhouses were not pleasant, so workers started to move to find work and were prepared to take lower pay, which clearly helped industry as the wage costs reduced. People moved into Stroud from the villages to find work or they would end up in the workhouse in Stroud. They also came from further afield, such as London. Thomas had moved from his home in Nympsfield to Rodborough, near Stroud, where there was more demand for his services. The valleys are known for their wool production and woollen mills; the period 1797 to 1834 saw a reduction of income for a hand-loom weaver from 26s a week to 5s a week, as labour rates fell.

The Combination Laws of 1800 had prevented men working together for a specific purpose: the intention had been to stop workers creating unions against the gentry and prevent the type of uprising seen in the French Revolution. But these laws stifled activity. Their modification in 1825 now allowed for business partnerships to be formed, thus creating an environment for businesses to be started by workers, as Thomas was to do with his sons.

In 1826 laws were changed and The Bank of England lost its position as the only joint stock bank and the promotion of joint stock companies was facilitated. This meant people with money could join together to create a "bank" to lend to business, or they could provide their capital directly to the business, subject to meeting certain legal directives. Previously, companies had to get a charter from Parliament. Initially, this was limited to certain trades but by 1862 it was extended to all trades. So rather than only funding business from profits generated, other investment capital could be brought in to grow a business faster.

There were other legislative changes that had an impact on businesses in Great Britain as a whole, and the Government were beginning to see that by encouraging free trade and a free market, the economy was improving. International trade was also improving, initially with members of the British Empire and then with France as it recovered from war. In 1815, exports were £51.8M; they fell to £31.5M, returning to £51.6M by 1841; by 1853 they had doubled to £98.9M.

The railway companies were a classic demonstration of men coming together to create businesses that were made possible by the new capital to make profit. In 1830 the railways began to extend rapidly; by 1848 188,000 navvies were involved in the construction, with a further 120,000 involved on preparing materials such as stone, brick and cement for erecting stations, building carriages and wagons, a total of 300,000. By 1850 this had increased to 600,000.

The railway to Stroud was opened in 1845 on the Swindon to Gloucester line by Great Western. A second line was built between Stonehouse and Nailsworth in 1867; privately constructed primarily as a goods line, it was taken over shortly after by the Midland Railway to join their main line at Stonehouse. In 1885 a further short section was built to a second station in Stroud. The line did not connect to the Great Western Line.

The Stroud valleys were famous for cloth manufacture. The surrounding hills were ideal for sheep and the valley streams allowed the introduction of mills through the 17th and 18th centuries. As a result, there were many wealthy mill owners who were looking for new ways of making money as the cloth, wool and cotton industries struggled in the later parts of the 19th century. The construction of the railway shows this local wealth being used to further the development of the area.

1853 to 1873 were known as the 'good years' for Great Britain. The railways brought great prosperity to towns & cities that were now connected; machine power was harnessed and transformed industry.

The building of the railway almost certainly benefited the Daniels business: contracts for its construction will have been awarded to local businesses and it will have needed cast parts for bridges, track, and stations. But Daniels was not the only iron foundry in the area: for instance, there was another at Dudbridge, only a mile away, but the project was probably large enough for them all to benefit and Daniels also could offer brasswork and machining, although they were still not very large at this time. However, in addition they definitely benefited from the better access by train to the rest of the country, with both increasing trade available in the valleys and orders from further afield. We also know that shortly afterwards Daniels invested in several other ventures, including a mill in the nearby village of Cam.

Until the mid-19th century, Engineering had been a trade that had not developed widely. Engines had been invented in the 18th century, but the take-up had been slow because they were built by hand, they were often unreliable and they sometimes didn't work at all; their build was a skill which was expensive and sometimes dangerous to get wrong. However, by the end of the 19th century machine tools were now being developed that could be used to manufacture parts far more accurately, to within one- thousandth of an inch, which made designs far easier to manufacture. Clearly, there was still skill, but it enabled blacksmiths, millwrights and carpenters throughout the land to start carrying out the new crafts of building engines and machines, and start employing lesser- skilled staff to build them.

This is not to say that Thomas Henry and Joseph were at the forefront; indeed, the growth of the business will have been limited initially by the availability of capital. Certainly it started as a simple blacksmith business and they were not businessmen in the early days; they were still involved primarily in their metalworking and foundry business. Early growth was generated primarily from profits, but the business continued to flourish and was not adversely affected by the Great Depression of 1873-1876, other than possibly the closure of the umbrella furniture manufacturer in which they had a share.

Chapter 6. The Move to Lightpill

By the 1870s the business had outgrown the space available at Church Place. A new site was found, a large field with a few old brick mill buildings located on the Bath Road between Rodborough and Lightpill. In addition, a cottage was adjacent to the site.

The brothers had sufficient funds from their existing business, the sale of the umbrella business, possibly a marriage dowry from the Isacke family, and from a loan to fund the new site. The land was sold to Thomas and Joseph in February 1875 by Samuel Baylis and the Trustees of the Tabernacle. The land had originally been owned by Samuel Jeffries, who owned the brick works on the bottom lane. The cottage was let to Joseph and Clara by Mr Alfred Apperley, later to be Sir Alfred Apperley, a gentleman who had inherited a family business that had made money over many years from cloth mills nearby. Alfred also owned Stringers Court and the estate located on the far side of Bath Road, above the site.

This is the first time we come across the Rodborough Tabernacle, a Congregational Free Church; both Joseph and Alfred were Congregationalists, taking an active part in the running of the church, but it plays a very big part in Daniels life, as we shall see later. Clara Ada came from a family whose ancestors were Baptists and embraced other religions; she herself was well educated and spoke other languages, so the connection with the Tabernacle may have been her influence.

The cottage, known as Fern Cottage, was a good size and allowed the couple to start a family, and provided space for Joseph to carry out his mechanical design activities.Thus Joseph set up the new facility whilst Thomas continued at Church Place, running the existing metal workshops.

Fern Cottage and the original brick mill buildings which were used for workshops and patten storage.

The site had some brick buildings already in existence that were used for workshops for making pattens, carrying out milling and storing work in progress. Open work sheds were constructed on an area below the house that was levelled.

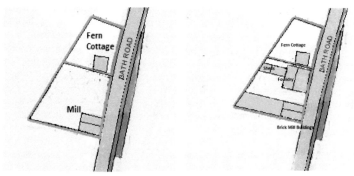

Fern Cottage on one plot, the mill site below. Developed as a foundry about 1870.

They initially set up a brass foundry on the new site. There were far fewer brass foundries than iron: at the time only three others were recorded in Gloucestershire. The advantages of brass were that it could be used for more finely detailed parts or for pieces where there was exposure to the elements and rusting could be a problem. It was therefore used for items requiring detail, such as church bells, small furniture hinges, door knobs, watch and clock parts, small engine and machine parts, piano string tensioners and decorative parts for walking sticks and car marques. In some applications it was necessary; in others it was seen as a luxury item that was afforded to only the wealthy. The metal was more expensive and the accuracy required was greater; thus it required more skill.

The site had some brick buildings already in existence that were used for workshops for making pattens, carrying out milling and storing work in progress.

Advances were also being made in iron and steel; early products such as baths, stoves and fireplaces were all made 'thick' to reduce the risk of shattering. The problem with this was that they were heavy to move around and used more material, which was expensive. But as technology improved, skilled founders were able to minimise the amount of material used and hence reduce the cost.

The technology in a brass foundry was more demanding than an iron foundry, the moulds or 'patterns' had to be more accurate and the risk of error was far greater. Daniels will have mastered these techniques in order to make the foundry a success.

As time went on, the site at Lightpill was developed, with buildings to house the increasing activity. The early buildings were around a yard directly below the

27

cottage. In time, additional buildings were added until there was very little space not occupied by buildings.

The original facility at Church Place was no longer required and was closed to concentrate on the new site, and Thomas moved to a house called Briarton, a house which still stands at the bottom of Walkeley Hill, which was nearer to the site of the foundry and workshops. In 1877 Thomas Henry married Elizabeth Martha Harris; originally from London, she was the daughter of Isaac Harris, a clerk in holy orders in Stroud. Thomas and Elizabeth moved again later in 1891 to a large house in Lansdown Road in Stroud, a location that now befitted his improved status as the business grew, away from the works, leaving Joseph to manage the operation. However, they kept Briarton House.

Briarton House; Fern Cottage extension.

In 1885 Fern Cottage was extended to the rear to house Joseph's growing family. The land above the house was kept as the family garden whilst the land below the house continued to be developed as the foundry.

The water supply was always an issue, because the foundry required a good supply of water for its operation, and in 1885 Alfred Apperley had a new well dug. The 67-foot well was dug out near to the house and three workmen were at work inside. They were removing the shuttering section by section and building the brick lining when Alfred's sons, who had been watching, shouted down to tell the men that the wall was collapsing. Only one man managed to escape; the other two became trapped under the weight of soil. A rescue attempt was launched and other men dug out the second man who, though shaken, was unharmed. Sadly, the third man was killed and his body retrieved the next day.

In April 1894 a further plot of land was bought from the Stroud Brewery Company between the existing site and The Fleece Inn. This enabled building to begin below the existing site, which was by then getting crowded.

28

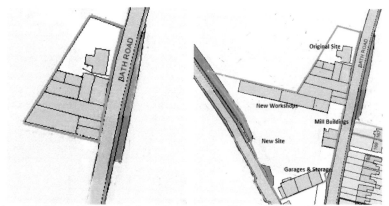

New Mill Site added to existing site developed from 1894 on land bought from Stroud Brewery.

Thomas Henry and Elizabeth had no children, leaving him time to devote to the business and hobbies. He became a pillar of society and member of many organisations including the Masons.

Freemasonry is such an old organisation that its true origins are uncertain; however, today's masonic rituals, terminology and symbolism are based around the ideas of stone masonry, a craft that goes back to ancient Egypt and before. Its coming into being as an organisation for non-practising masons is thought to have been around the Crusades, which would agree with its ideals of chivalry. In essence, a mason is someone who is 'just and upright' and adheres to morals.

Traditionally, 'gentlemen' were often members of clubs, where they could do business with other 'gentlemen', but for many new businessmen of the 18th and 19th century, this opportunity eluded them. A masonic club, where members learned how to be good pillars of society through role-play of traditional rituals, whilst meeting other businessmen, was invaluable. A process called 'blackballing' ensured that 'rogues' were excluded!

One primary purpose of Masonry is to 'do good' through community service and fundraising. Today, Masonry is one of the biggest fundraising charities in the country, and so it was then. Members believed in putting 'good' back into the community, and this is something in which the Daniels believed through their Christian upbringing. It was this 'sense of duty' to look after others that was to be with them through the whole period of the company's existence.

But there was a side effect to the organisation outside of the normal meetings. In the Stroud valleys, wealth had been amassed as a result of cotton, wool and cloth production in the 16th & 17th centuries. Banking and banks were still in their infancy, and were not a major part in providing money to help small businesses start and grow. Masonry enabled businessmen to meet with like-minded individuals and facilitated the introduction of capital from wealthy business owners into the new technical and engineering businesses that would make the future profits. In addition, members could work together in business outside of the lodge, secure in the knowledge that they shared a common bond. In Masonry they would share a common belief in 'a gentleman's word', important if you are to provide money or contracts to someone else's business.

During the Industrial Revolution the number of Masonic Lodges in Great Britain, and indeed across the world, rapidly increased, a sign of their importance. Details of meetings were regularly posted in newspapers. Parts of the modern-day ceremony date back to a time when processions were held in public streets and it was an open organisation. Only in later years did it change, when the Masons in Germany were persecuted during the war, and later still when it became frowned upon as an organisation where business was done behind closed doors. It is a shame that we now rely on our banks as the main route to finance!

Thomas Henry was a mason for twenty years and was very active, putting in many hours' service, but it may have been that Masonry served a dual purpose for him and, in addition to the enjoyment of the ceremonial activities, it gave him a standing in the business community, and may have helped with access to funding for the business and contacts for sales.

Funding growth was critical for the 'new' businesses, and is the reason that most businesses at this time were started by people who already had wealth and contacts. So Daniels will have needed to work at building their network. In addition, it was not unusual for businesses at the earlier stage of the supply chain to provide 'credit', in exchange for a shareholding in the customer's business or as a loan secured against the customer's property.

Joseph, on the other hand, did not join the Masons but he did join Rodborough Parish Council and was involved in it for many years. Alfred Apperley was another councillor. In addition, Joseph supported the Stroud Fire Service and attended the annual fundraising dinners. The service was created and primarily supported by the businesses in the area.

Large cast wheels about 1898.

Meanwhile, the funding was enabling Daniels to expand rapidly as local demand for cast iron and steelwork grew in the late 19th century. The foundry was able to produce bigger and bigger pieces of work with an increasing focus on business needs rather than household goods, which had been a staple. The men could turn their hands to the production of many products. Also, the capabilities of the mechanical design and draughtsmen, and the lathes and tools in the workshops provided a 'one stop shop' for customers. Companies operating in Stroud were keen to have machines to mechanise processes, thus reduce labour costs and enable them to increase market share and increase profit. But often they had little knowledge of design or machinery, and so a company capable of producing what they needed was of great benefit. Daniels had a reputation for quality and a foundry capable of producing from the smallest to the largest of items.

Wheels and cogs for use in machines. A 300lb pressure, gas-fired boiler.

Wheels and cogs were commonly used in machinery such as in the mills, but machines were developed by Daniels to do everything, from making hairpins to washing clothes. Daniels were involved in a vast variety of different machines: grindstones, valves, pumps, lathes for turning wood, saw benches, moulding machines, screw strap guides – the list seems endless.

Hairpin machine & mortar mill from 1898.

Design was carried out, drawings produced and a patten was made; this was basically a 'model' of the part. In the earlier days it was usually of wood that was carved; in later years it was metal, worked by machine to create the form required. This 'model' could then be used to press into a block of sand to leave an imprint. This then formed the mould for the molten metal to be poured into. Once the first of a machine had been produced, the patten was indexed and stored so that if another was required for another customer, it could be easily reproduced. By the turn of the century, Daniels had over 3,000 pattens and re-produced many machines to the same design. Most of the work was 'one-offs', but sometimes orders would be received for a dozen hairpin machines or cloth washers for bigger companies.

From 1899 a cloth steaming pot with a crane. Notice the scale provided by the man on the left. A series of cloths are draped rather unsuccessfully to provide a backdrop; a cloth washer from 1899; an umbrella-notching machine from 1899.

32

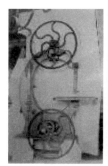  

Machines including peat firelighter cutting machine, 1905.

'West Gigs' machine for cloth production under construction in 1903, and 'volume production' of walking stick bending machines..

Japanning stove, 1904, used to produce lacquer work furniture in the Japanese style; Waterwheel for Gloucester, 1901.

33

Despite the huge number of machines made at the site, there are now few examples of cast ironwork produced by the Lightpill Ironworks from this period still in existence; however, I am aware of some iron columns in the Malt House at the Cirencester Brewery Maltings, Cricklade Street, Cirencester, believed to date to 1880, each inscribed:

T.H. & J. DANIELS/IRONFOUNDERS/STROUD.

In some respects Daniels was not unique. At this time, companies throughout the land were also carrying out similar activities and industrial development was flourishing.

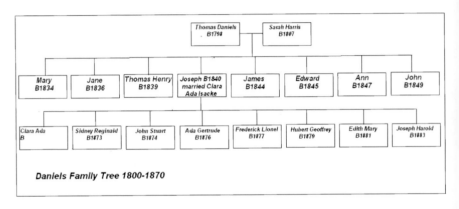

Daniels Family Tree 1800-1870

1892. Joseph and Clara Ada with children (Clara Ada (20), Herbert Geoffrey (13), Joseph Harold (9), John Stuart (18), Father, Mother, Edith Mary (7)

34

Clara Ada was the first daughter of Joseph and Clara Ada, born in 1872. She went on to be well educated, going to Stratford Abbey to be taught by her mother's sisters, the Isackes, at their school. Sidney Reginald was their eldest son and went to Wycliffe College, as we shall see later.

In 1897, Alfred Apperley's second son, Francis William, married Clara Ada, eldest daughter of Joseph. Francis was a mechanical engineer and they lived for five years in Rodborough before moving to Shoreditch in London and then to Middlesex.

The Apperley family were well respected in the area. They owned the Dubridge Mill that dated back to the twelfth century. By 1832 it was occupied by John Apperley, whose business was carried on after 1834 by his sons, James and David. The firm became one of the most successful in the region, gaining many awards for its cloth, including a gold medal at the 1851 Exhibition. An iron foundry was set up on the south-west side of the main road before 1863 by James Apperly, known as the Dudbridge Ironworks. It was a firm set up to manufacture his patent clothmaking machinery, but was sold in 1871 and the same business was carried on by Cooke, Vick & Co.

From 1872 the cloth-making business was headed by David's son, Alfred Apperly, later Sir Alfred, and it was made a limited company, under the name of Apperly, Curtis & Co. The Apperleys were shrewd investors: it was their cottage which was first used by Joseph as the start of the iron foundry at Lightpill, and they may well have invested in the business. 1901 records show that the T.H. & J. business had received ninety-seven different personal loans in its history; six remained outstanding, the largest of which, £900, was from a C.A. which may well have been Charles Apperley, Alfred's first son who ran the cloth-making business by then. Joseph Daniels and Alfred Apperley were well acquainted: they were both involved in Rodborough Tabernacle, both Governors of Rodborough School and the Fire Service.

Bridge with a span of 40 foot.

Chapter 7. Machine Tools.

"a good deal of metal turning was done with hand or treadle lathes and recounting the devices that were used to turn out very heavy work with inadequate appliances"

This was part of a speech given by John Stewart Daniels in 1950, at the time of the celebration of 100 years of the company, recounting his childhood memories of the business around the turn of the century. He recounts that it was very much a "family affair", with his father and uncle running the business and then he and his brothers entering the business. He recounts how much the business relied on the skills of the workers to produce the parts required on machines that were not designed for the work – in the early days, the machines that were powered by the operator with a foot treadle.

Traditionally, lathes date back many hundreds of years, but the greatest period for lathe development was also around the turn of the century, the period to which the speech refers; and it was the development of 'machine tools', in part pioneered by Alfred Herbert in the UK, that had a dramatic impact on British engineering development and created what was known at the time as the Second Industrial Revolution.

A lathe in use in Daniels and an advert for Alfred Herbert lathes.

Alfred was born in 1866, the son of a wealthy landowner. He attended a private school and was destined for university, but his school friend, William Hubbard, had started work at Joseph Jessops Engineering Co. in Leicester, working on a lathe. Albert was fascinated by the lathe and persuaded his father to let him serve an apprenticeship at Jessops. After completion he moved on to Coles & Mathews and became a manager for the company, producing machinery for the cycle trade; his brother, William, owned the Premier Cycle Co., and guaranteed the company orders.

In 1888 Alfred bought the company from the owners and, together with his good friend, William, started to develop a range of drilling machines and hand lathes. A year later Alfred changed the name to 'Herbert Machine Tools', and embarked on a design programme that included milling machines, cutter grinders, capstan lathes and special machinery for the cycle industry. The business was also underpinned by the import and sales of French tubing for use in the cycle industry.

Bicycles were in great demand and designs were quickly improving. Coventry became the leading region in the UK for development and manufacture, and this resulted in a huge demand for machine tools. The advances in tools meant that designs could be repeated accurately; tolerances could be calculated, ensuring that parts could be machined and would always fit together. Then in 1899 a high- speed steel was developed that revolutionised the industry: instead of forging and grinding individual tools, they could be produced from HSS, which resulted in minimising tool wear so that the results were vastly improved. The invention, credited to an American company, was pioneered by companies in Sheffield, and by 1905 British makers exported the new cutting tools all over the world.

Accuracy in manufacture was of greatest importance when building complex and large designs containing many parts and when tolerances are critical for operation. Nowhere is this more true than in engine manufacture, and the advent of HSS paved the way for the development of motor cars, with the cycle industry forming the basis for development.

	No of Firms	No in Midlands	Output of leading firms	% Herbert's
1870	131	12	32,238	
1890	228	22	227,481	3.5
1900	315	53	497,648	25.7
1913	250	64	1,219,878	42.1

Source: Floud British Machine Tool Industry.

Coventry became a centre for motor car development, and although Herberts had diversified into supplying tools to a wide range of industries, including the munitions industry that was later to become of great importance to the company, it was cars that afforded the meteoric rise in the business. By the start of the First World War, Herberts were one of only seventeen machine tool companies and had achieved a 42.1% share.

Chapter 8. Cam Mills

The Daniels brothers' efforts were focused on the business. Money was always tight as it was required to grow the company, but in 1888, around the time Thomas joined the Masons and was becoming recognized for his business, Thomas and Joseph went into partnership with some others to start a corn mill.

The brothers bought the mill, but the other partners pulled out through a lack of finance, leaving them with an empty factory. At the time, the traditional cloth businesses were going through a difficult period, with reduced prices and less demand. In addition, it was not a business that the brothers knew much about, but the Old Mill buildings represented good value, providing a lot of space without huge capital outlays. It was in the village of Cam to the south of Stroud near Dursley.

The development of new machines had transformed the shoe industry, from a cottage industry with a 'cobbler' hand making shoes to order in every village to the production of shoes cut up and stitched together on machines in a factory environment. The reducing costs of production resulted in cheaper shoes, and demand increased as people were able to afford more than one pair. However, the shoe soles were made of leather, and sheep farming was going through a difficult time, under pressure from imports of wool. One problem the industry faced was the waste once the soles had been cut from the leather. Daniels developed machines that could cut up and pulp the waste. The irregularly laid leather fibres, each having a different skeleton substance, were bonded using natural animal glues, readily available locally; the pulp was then pressed into boards that dried to a firm material that showed leather-like qualities that could be cut to create soles. This was then used in the shoe industry as a cheaper alternative to whole leather pieces in the soles. Once the soles were cut from the board, the waste from this could then go back into the process to form more board.

The leather offcuts were inexpensive 'waste' that was in ready supply in the Stroud region; the machinery was designed and built in the Daniels factory and so the cost of starting the enterprise was low. In time, the advantage of space in the mill was better utilised. Larger machines produced bigger boards with less waste, and could be operated by a small number of staff; indeed, the operation was not labour-intensive. The space enabled leather and board to be stored. And so they started a leather-board business in the Middle Mills.

Shoe production became more mechanised but was not fully automated; as a result, the manufacturing became more centralised in cities where there was greater availability of cheap labour. The people of Stroud were becoming more educated, and the shortage of flat land limited the building of cheap housing. Fortunately, the board was fairly light and easy to transport; the arrival of the railway to the factory by 1898 enabled transport of the board, and companies around Leicester became an important market for the company.

Manufacturing the board machine for Cam

By 1902 the Daniels Board Mill had a turnover of £4,250, a sum that was not far short of the engineering business's, but was achieved with a single basic product that required less manpower and less management effort. The business was virtually autonomous of the main engineering business.

Middle Mills, Cam, 1899.

Middle Mills, Cam, 1899, from the railway siding.

The core activity of the main business was design engineering and manufacture. They designed machines for other businesses to enable them to increase production, cut costs and aid manufacture. They were probably instrumental in supporting the development of every industry in the area at some stage with machines, and helped fuel the growth of Stroud. They also provided one-off engineering solutions such as bridges and wheels.

So the Mills was a rare venture where they developed machines for their own production to supply a product to an end customer and Cam was to prove a highly successful venture over the coming years.

41

Chapter 9. The Isacke Family

Joseph Daniels married Clara Ada Isacke, so our next 'root' of the family history concerns the Isacke family, whom we can trace back to a Richard Ysac born in Foston, Lincolnshire in the 1500's. The name "Isacke" as used in the recent past is believed to originate from the Jewish name 'Isaac', and differing versions appear in records, including Isaac and Isack. The family Bible records a decision for a name change in 1667 to drop the "e", so the changes may not have always been accidental. A name with Jewish origin is likely to have been changed at times in history.

Five generations of the family made their homes in South Lincolnshire before Sutton Isacke, christened in 1638, moved away from his home in Great Gonerby to seek a career in London. In 1655, at the age of seventeen, he became apprentice to Thomas Knifton, the famed lantern clockmaker based in the heart of the City of London in Lothbury. The industry was relatively new, the Clockmakers' Guild having started in only 1633. In 1662 Sutton was admitted as a 'free clockmaker' and was able to set up on his own. He married Jeanne Harvey and had a daughter, Elizabeth, in 1664, christened in the Old Jewry in the centre of the City and adjacent to Lothbury.

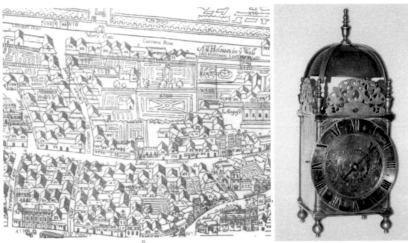

Map of London Showing Old Jewry and a Knifton Clock

The 'Jewry' was the Jewish area of London, leading us to believe that the Isackes were by this time still of the Jewish faith. London was liberal in its views towards the Jewish faith, unlike many other areas of Europe at the time when Catholicism created anti-sematic sentiment, and Jews were not allowed trades in

42

new goods, could not own land, and were confined to the Jewry after dark. This was not the case in London.

In 1665 the plague struck London and the area around. The Old Jewry was badly affected. The clockmaking industry was decimated. Plague victims were isolated in their houses with their families to try to prevent the spread of disease. Sutton left London, taking his daughter with him, and set sail for St Helena; there is no mention of his wife, so the likelihood is that she had died of the plague and he left to escape before he died too. It proved to be a sound move because the area in which he lived and worked was decimated by the Great Fire a year later, and little still survives today.

St Helena, a small island off the west coast of Africa, was a useful stopping point for ships passing around the Cape of Africa. It had experienced an eventful history, passing from ownership of the Spanish, Portuguese and British, until the British decided to populate it and offered free passage and land to those who would like to emigrate from London.

Sutton married again in 1667, soon after his arrival on the island, to Elizabeth. They settled in Fisher's Valley on the east side of the island, three or four miles from the capital, Jamestown, and near the location of the airport that is now built there. The East India Company, on behalf of the British Government, had divided the island into one hundred and fifty portions of land for planters to start; but the hills around the valley resulted in scorching hot summers and misty, windy tropical winters which were more conducive to the raising of cattle than growing crops, and so Sutton became a cattle farmer.

Sutton and Elizabeth settled and raised a family comprising Susanna, Naomi, Michael, Leah and Sutton. Sutton senior died in 1715. Times were probably tough. In Sutton senior's will, made in 1713, as well as leaving his estate to Sutton junior, he left 'all my wearing apparel' to Thomas Collier, his grandson. The family owned part of an area called Longwood, where one of the cattle sheds was later remodelled into a house. The house was used by the Governor as his summer residence until 1815, when it was used to house Napoleon Bonaparte and his entourage when he was exiled by the British until his death in 1820. The house is now restored and forms a museum of the Napoleonic era.

Sutton junior married Penelope Miller and had a family of nine children, again mostly girls. The eldest son, Sutton, born in 1716, decided to move back to England, where he married Ann Stanton in 1744 in London, and started a career as a brush-maker.

Chapter 10. Mormons and Brush-Making

Sutton's son George was born in 1768 in London. George married Susannah and had a large family. The family by now were Baptists and most of the sons were becoming skilled 'brush makers'.

Their fourth son, James was born in 1799. He married Hannah Mitchell Draper, who was born in Stroud and so he moved to Stroud to set up his own brush making business. James & Hannah had a family of six children, one of whom, Clara Ada, married Joseph Daniels.

Mr & Mrs James Isacke, parents of Clara Ada.

Some of the Isacke family were well educated, Clara Ada was later known as the best linguist in Gloucestershire, and together with her sisters, set-up a school in Stroud as we shall see later. The family were business people, running brush making concerns employing workers. But we do not know how they became educated.

However there are several detailed accounts of their lives and letters written that ended up in the Church of the Latter Day Saints archive in Salt Lake City. This has helped to provide the account of ordinary life for other parts of the family within this chapter as well as more detail about the lives of James & Hannah in Stroud, and shows that they were not wealthy, indeed in most respects a family in poverty but staunchly religious.

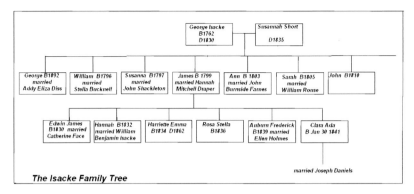

		George Isacke B1762 D1830		Susannah Short D1835		

George B1892 married Addy Eliza Diss	William B1796 married Stella Bucknell	Susanna B1797 married John Shackleton	James B 1799 married Hannah Mitchell Draper	Ann B 1803 married John Burnside Farnes	Sarah B1805 married William Rouse	John B1810

Edwin James B1830 married Catherine Face	Hannah B1832 married William Benjamin Isacke	Harriette Emma B1834 D1862	Rosa Stella B1836	Auburn Frederick B1839 married Ellen Holmes	Clara Ada B Jan 30 1841

married Joseph Daniels

The Isacke Family Tree

Now James's sister Ann married John Burnside Farnes, a bookbinder by trade, who enjoyed playing the violin. They had their first child, Mary Ann, in 1830, just three and a half months after they married. George, Ann's father, died in the same year.

They had seven children over the next nine years, but times were tough. Ebenezer received only six weeks' formal education; Matilda fell ill at eleven months, 'which caused her to differ from other children', and Matthew was bitten by a dog, which left scars on both sides of his face and resulted in his having a beard in later life.

When Ebenezer was about six years old and out with his brothers, he fell into the canal; passers-by seeing him fortunately saved him from drowning by fishing him out with an umbrella. It was cold and his clothes were frozen by the time he reached home.

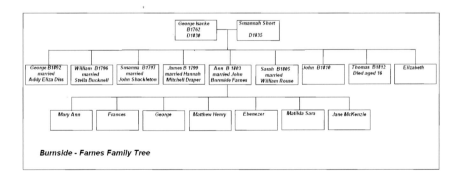

			George Isacke B1762 D1830	Susannah Short D1835				

George B1892 married Addy Eliza Diss	William B1796 married Stella Bucknell	Susanna B1797 married John Shackleton	James B 1799 married Hannah Mitchell Draper	Ann B 1803 married John Burnside Farnes	Sarah B1805 married William Rouse	John B1810	Thomas B1812 Died aged 16	Elizabeth

Mary Ann	Frances	George	Matthew Henry	Ebenezer	Matilda Sara	Jane McKenzie

Burnside - Farnes Family Tree

45

John crushed his leg in an accident that resulted in his being unable to work for thirteen months, during which time they were too poor to pay for a doctor, and there were great strains on the family budget. This resulted in the children's working from about the age of eight: Mary Ann worked for a wealthy family; George worked in a silk factory making fringe; Matthew served a tinsmith apprenticeship; Ebenezer served as a messenger boy, a printer's devil and a dry goods clerk, whilst Matilda worked for Governors & Chatters at 86 Cannon Street West.

To set the world scene: in America in the 1820's Joseph Smith (1805-1844), a poor Vermont-born son of a schoolmaster, claimed as a teenager to have been visited by the angel Moroni and shown the location of a buried set of gilded plates. When, at the age of twenty-one, he was 'allowed' to rescue them from their burial place near the family home in upstate New York, he discovered, along with the leaves, a pair of crystal spectacles (better described as a pair of 'seeing' stones) which translated the 'Reformed Egyptian' hieroglyphics into English redolent of the King James Bible. As the angel had forbidden him to show the plates to anyone, and in fact later 'reclaimed' them, he dictated the translation initially to his young wife, but later to a well-off farmer, who funded their publication, in March 1830, as the Book of Mormon. Some days later, the church was established – a strong, paternalist theocracy with Joseph as its leader.

By 1832 he had won over 1,000 converts, but not all of the public were pleased and his 'organisation' had to relocate several times before eventually settling in Salt Lake City in spring 1846, following a great trek across the plains using specially built wagons.

In Britain, the British Mormon Mission started in 1837. Britain was wealthier than the US and Smith saw this as a base to draw capital to fund the community as well as labour.

In January 1850, Sutton Isacke, Ann's brother, was baptized into the faith and, with the enthusiasm of a new convert, began spending his evenings visiting people and carrying the message of the restoration. In February, brother William was baptized, but sadly died just two years later. Ann was a religious person, but played no active part in a Christian church, unlike many of her family. Offered the opportunity of curing her asthma, she too converted in April. It was said that her asthma was instantly cured.

Next was his sister Susannah. Widowed at an early age, she struggled to support her five children. She was a staunch Baptist and taught the children to read, using the Bible, reading a chapter every morning. They regularly attended church and Sunday School. Her daughter Ellen was ill for weeks with inflammatory rheumatism and was not expected to live; Sutton had been invited to come to say some farewell prayers for her. But he said some 'prayer as they had never heard before' and when he rose to his feet he said that she would get better and they would become

Mormons and go to 'Zion', the promised land that was Salt Lake City, Utah. She recovered soon afterwards.

During the 1850's there were up to 8,000 baptisms a year into the Mormon Church in the UK with over 2,000 a year immigrating to America. Of surprise in the 1851 census was that there were 222 meeting places, with a following estimated in the region of 25-30,000. The greatest surge was in the period of the Crimean War 1853-6. By 1870 24% of the population of Utah were of British birth and 80% were Mormons.

Over the next few years more members of the family converted amid stories of great illnesses being resolved by visits from Mormon Elders, and eventually even John, Ann's husband, relented. And so it naturally followed that the attraction of the Promised Land took hold and on 18 February 1856, daughter Mary Ann, with her husband Samuel Woods House, set sail from Liverpool Harbour aboard the ship Caravan, to New York and ultimately destined for Utah. During the voyage, amid a violent storm, Mary Ann gave birth to a daughter, to be her only one, named Ellen Caravan House. For a year they lived in New York before moving to Chicago and it wasn't until 1859 that they finally made the journey across the Great Plains to Utah.

In 1860, George, now twenty-one, and Matthew, nineteen, set sail from Liverpool and arrived in Utah by the 'fall', joining their sister in the village of Grantsville. Next was sister Frances, who had married John F Reed and had moved to Scotland in 1860 to spread the Mormon faith and serve the Church. In 1861 they completed their assignment and emigrated with their children, Frances Ann, Selina, Helen Matilda and John McKenzie, together with John's sister, Sarah Reed. Then in 1862, Ebenezer, nineteen, set sail on his journey across the Atlantic and thence on to Salt Lake City, working his passage as a cook aboard a train.

Finally, in 1863, Ann, now aged fifty-nine, sailed with John, aged fifty-six, children Matilda and Jane, together with Sutton and his wife Martha, niece Ellen Shackleton and John Lyons, the son of family friends, who, aged only three, was never to know his parents.

The voyage was made more important by the arrival of a reporter for the *Uncommercial Traveller*, a certain Charles Dickens, who was most impressed, and wrote a long article on the conditions aboard ship and the people about to embark upon their long and scary voyage.

Susannah Shackleton, Ellen's mother, was last to emigrate with her son, George, in 1864. She sold all she owned in London and put her remaining possessions in a sack for the journey. Sadly, they were all stolen, leaving her penniless and broken-hearted. She died the same year in the arms of her daughter, Annie, having been just re-united.

47

But the story of the Daniels family is more concerned with those remaining in Britain. James moved to Stroud and had set up a brush, clog and pattern-making business by 1830 in Nelson Street. He met his wife, Hannah Mitchel, who was from Gloucester. His brother George, married to Addy, had five sons: George, William, Henry, Chas, James and John. Sadly, George had died early in 1830, at the age of thirty-eight, leaving Addy to bring up the children. James and John had gone to live with their Uncle James in Stroud, and by 1841 James had joined Uncle James in the brush-making business. His son, James Edwin, became his apprentice. By 1861 he was employing six men and his son Auburn Frederick had joined the business.

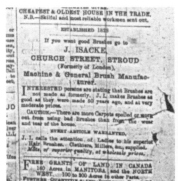

Advert in Stroud Citizen 1882, the school.

His daughters Hannah and Harriet had become teachers, well paid in those days. This may have helped Rosa and Clara Ada to become principals and set up their own school. In 1870 a boarding school for girls was opened in the old Stratford Abbey. In 1871 there were fourteen pupils and a reasonable teaching staff in place. How much input Hannah and Harriet provided is unclear, but the school thrived with many boarding pupils from London, presumably through family connections. Aunt Sarah Rouse worked for an Account Book Manufacturers for many years in London and visited the family in Stroud in the summer for many years.

Chapter 11. John Isacke

'To enjoy the delights of the sunny hour
Afar in the forest I love to stray,
Where the wild birds warble their woodland lay
'Midst scenes of the deepest solitude,
Where scarcely a foot has been known t'intrude,
Where the snake may bask with his speckled crest,
And the raven croak from her high built nest,
And swift from the brake the coney bound,
To sport without fear on its native ground,

Afar in the forest I love to stray,
Where the wild flowers bloom on the pathless way,
And far o'er the woodland blend their sweets
To fill with perfume those sequester'd   retreats,
Where the ivy aloft round the oak doth cling
And the wild bee wanders on restless wing,
And the butterfly flutters from flower to flower,
To enjoy the delights of the sunny hour."

                                           John Isacke, 1859

James's brother, John, had also moved away from London and relocated to Stroud. He also was a brush-maker by trade and may well have moved up to work with James in his flourishing business. But his main interest was in writing poetry.

In 1854 the church burial grounds in Stroud were becoming so full, and the risks of disease to the crowded town so great, that it was decided to create a new cemetery on the outskirts of the town. The site chosen was to the east, on the Bisley Road, and John became the curator of the cemetery, living in a small, new cottage at the entrance. This suited him ideally as it afforded him time to dedicate to his writing activities in a location in a countryside setting, the grounds that were beautifully landscaped by a local nurseryman. This was a position that he was to hold until his death in 1873. Ironically, he was not buried in the cemetery, but in the Daniels family graveyard at the church in Rodborough, having been tended in sickness by his niece, Clara Ada in the Daniels home in Rodborough.

Sadly, he died single, although a letter written much later from Clara to the relatives in America says that there was 'a young woman Uncle John was going to marry'; maybe his love was 'Laura', who appears in his poem *Contrition, written to Laura*.

I believe that the influences of his sadness and loneliness and the setting at the cemetery can be seen in some of his works. These poems are taken from his book:

142.   And others in the bed of death,
        Have calmly laid them down to sleep,
        No more to smell thy perfum'd breath.
        Or wander o'er the pleasant heath,
        Or down thy zigzag creep.

        For destiny of human life,
        None ever yet on Earth could trace;
        Or change the everflowing strife,
        (Naught but an angel staid the knife,)
        In holy Abraham's case.

        And thus despite of all our fears,
        A guardian hand is o'er us spread,
        Which silently the spirit cheers.
        Dispels the gloom and dries our tears.
        When hope has nearly fled.

        The Sun it smiles as bright today
        As when we first beheld its light;
        The woods are green, the flowers as gay,
        And Nature dress' d in rich array,
        Still please the ravished sight.

        Children are sporting on the green,
        As gay as we were wont to be,
        How animating is the scene –
        But let a few years intervene.
        And banished is their glee.

        The changes of a few short years
        The pleasing visions thus destroy;
        So strange, so mystic it appears.
        It brings the eye suffused with tears,
        Instead of smiling joy.

143.   Then let us seek not, doubt or fear,
        For those we own are truly blest,
        "Who patiently their course" will steer,
        The few short years they journey here;
        Then wait "the promised rest."

50

He had an exhibition of his work in Stroud at the Institute, possibly in 1841, and the book of his works was published in 1859, entitled *Leisure hours, a collection of poems.*

'Leisure hours' by John Isacke; the Roman Pavement photographed by John Stuart at the opening ceremony.

Few of the places around the Stroud valleys are specifically mentioned, except for the Roman Pavement at Woodchester:

> BEHOLD what wonders now delight our eyes
> As here we view the scenes of ancient days,
> Presenting forms which fill us with surprise.
>
> As with fond curiosity we gaze;
> The pile is razed, but spite of spoil's bereavement
> Time has still spared the Tesselated Pavement.

The cemetery continues to inspire today's artists: this photograph by Shirley Margerison was taken in the cemetery and forms part of an exhibition that was held in the Gate House in 2009, where John lived.

In 1873 John was surprised to receive a letter from his sister Ann, who was by now in Salt Lake City, Utah. As well as finding out about the family, she was interested to find out more of their ancestry. He wrote a letter in response and it tells the story of how, after James's wife Hannah had died in 1866, he had decided to marry again, a lady very much younger. This caused great family upheaval particularly as he had intended not to tell his offspring as this excerpt states:

'He told his eldest daughter (Hannah) Draper when she was coming away, he hoped she would never darken his door again. Clara (Ada) and Rosa (Stella) are keeping a boarding school. He never told them when he went off to get married, but they found out, and while he was gone they removed their boxes and what belonged to them out of the house, and on his return he accused them of robbing his house and abused them very much. So that they have had nothing to do with him ever since. He then fell out with Auburn Frederick, his son, who, after leaving him and laying about for a twelve month or more, started out for America where he fell in with Aunt Smith (his mother's sister) and finally married the adopted daughter of his Aunt.'

From letters sent by Clara we know that the rift with James, her father, was to heal. He died in December 1884, and Clara was visiting him regularly through his illness after he suffered a stroke earlier in the month. But when he died, he was taken to the cemetery and not afforded a position in the Daniels plot as her uncle had been given.

Chapter 12. British Rule in India

Sidney Reginald was born on 18 September 1873. He was the eldest son of Joseph and Clara Ada and was born in Fern Cottage, the cottage on the main Bath Road out of Stroud that was later to be on the site where the factories were later built. He was clearly bright. The family believed in good education, his mother having started and run a school in Stroud, and now they had sufficient funds so that he was the first Daniels member to be able to be funded to attend a private school.

The school chosen for his education was Wycliffe College in nearby Stonehouse, where he was able to attend as a day pupil. This was the start of a relationship between the Daniels family and the school that was to last for many years.

Joseph's sister Eliza had married William S. Harrison and was living in Kings Stanley. William was also a wheelwright & carpenter. Joseph was fully engaged running the engineering business; his wife, who was in a partnership running her girls' boarding school at Stratford Abbey was also clearly busy, and so it was left to other members of the family to help out.

As a result, Joseph and Eliza's sister Jane lived with sister Eliza in Kings Stanley and looked after Joseph and Clara Ada's children: John Stuart, Ada Gertrude, Frederickk Lionel, Hubert Geoffrey and, of course, Sidney Reginald.

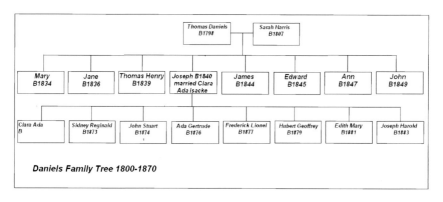

Daniels Family Tree 1800-1870

This arrangement was convenient for Sidney and John to be day pupils at Wycliffe since it was much closer to the school. But it was a boys' school and so Ada was not part of this educational arrangement.

Sidney did well at school, was a top scholar and succeeded in achieving a place at Balliol College in Oxford to study Law. From here he went on to London University and passed his barristers' exams to enable him to become a member of the judiciary. In 1891 he applied for and was successful in joining the Civil Service.

In 1893 he passed the exam for the Indian Civil Service and left that year to work in India.

A group of students at Balliol College at the time Sidney was at the College, 1892-93; the college in 1890.

Indian rule at this time was complex. The East India Company had operated under legal charter from the British Government as a trading company since the 1700's. They had increased the lands under British jurisdiction through the clever manipulation of the native Indian tribes and the use of their 'army' of locals, paid for from trading profits at no cost to the British taxpayer. A succession of leaders including Clive of India ruled over 'British' land, using company law that increased to cover the majority, though not all, of India.

The British Government, not happy with the situation, was virtually powerless because their armies were already overstretched fighting in other regions of the Empire and there was no money available for the additional responsibilities of India. But the Industrial Revolution in Britain provided sufficient funds in the 1830's, allowing the British Government to appoint their own dignitaries to India. These new leaders brought with them the belief that India should be ruled under British Law, regardless of local tribal laws and beliefs. This resulted in increasing unrest and friction with the more liberal East India Company Law and ultimately triggered riots in 1856. The result was that the East India Company was disbanded in 1857.

The North-West Provinces were the last great region to come into British control during the East India Company campaigns.

British India

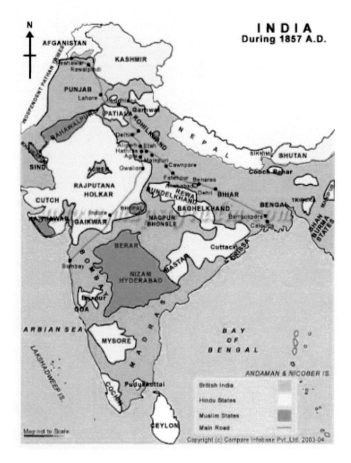

Lord Wellesley,Governor-General, arrived in India in 1797 and progressively obtained from the Nawab of Oudh the cession of Rohilkhand, the lower Doab, and the Gorakhpur Division, thus enclosing Awadh on all sides except the north. In 1804, as the result of Lord Lake's victories in the Second Anglo-Maratha War, part of Bundelkhand and the rest of the Doab, including Agra and the guardianship of the old and blind emperor, Shah Alam, at Delhi, were obtained from Scindia. In 1815 the Kumaon Division was acquired after the Gurkha War, and a further portion of Bundelkhand from the Maratha Peshwa in 1817. These new acquisitions, known as the ceded and conquered provinces, continued to be administered by the Governor-General as part of Bengal. In 1833 an Act of Parliament was passed to constitute a new presidency (province), with its capital at Agra. But this scheme was never fully carried out, and in 1835 another statute authorized the appointment of a Lieutenant-Governor for the North-Western Provinces, as they were then known.

The North-Western Provinces included the Delhi and Gurgaon territories, transferred later, after the Revolt of 1857 to the Punjab; and also (after 1853) the Saugor and Nerbudda Territories, which in 1861 became part of the Central Provinces. Awadh remained under its Nawab, who was permitted to assume the title of King in 1819. Awadh was annexed in 1856 and constituted a separate chief commissionership. Then followed the Revolt of 1857, when all signs of British rule were for a time swept away throughout the greater part of the two provinces. The Lieutenant-Governor died when shut up in the fort at Agra, and Oudh was only reconquered after several campaigns lasting for eighteen months.

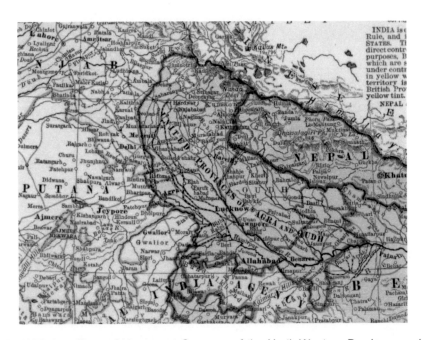

In 1877 the offices of Lieutenant-Governor of the North-Western Provinces and Chief Commissioner of Oudh were combined in the same person; and in 1902, when the new name of United Provinces of Agra and Oudh was introduced, the title of chief commissioner was dropped, though Oudh still retained some marks of its former independence. In 1935, the name of the province was shortened to the United Provinces. It stretched from the Great Plains around Allahabad and Lucknow in the east, to Delhi and Agra in the west. In the north-west was desert, to

56

the north the mountains of Tibet, and to the south the mountains. Parts of the region were agricultural, producing rice and other crops, but other areas in the west were barren and wild. It was in this region that the 1857 uprisings occurred, and there continued to be resistance through the ensuing period of British Governance.

And it was to this region that Sidney Reginald was posted in 1893.

The East India Company had operated from supreme courts in Calcutta, Madras and Bombay. These courts were only concerned with major offences, minor offences being handled 'on horseback' at grass roots level. But the British Government needed to create a more structured approach and so in 1861 the Indian High Courts Act passed by British Parliament established high courts in other places. In 1866, the High Court of Judicature for the North-West Provinces came into existence at Agra. In 1869 the High Court was shifted from Agra to Allahabad.

Sidney spent thirty-seven years in India as a judge. How much freedom for operation he received from the outset is supposition, but certainly the Civil Service was an all-British affair, the only entry method through an exam sat in the UK. He would have been valued for his up-to-date knowledge of the latest laws and methodology.

His first assignment was to Jalaun, a small place 100 miles South West of Lucknow as Assistant Magistrate, then Etah, Shahjahan, Meerut and so on until by 1899 he had become Joint Magistrate, the assigned towns having risen to ten. He had no break from service to return home until 1902 when in May he returned to Great Britain.

Sidney in Oxford about 1894, Caroline, Sidney's first wife.

Many civil servants took Indian wives but Sidney did not. Whether it might have caused local difficulties for a member of the judiciary, I don't know. But during his return to Britain in 1903 he married Caroline Hutchings. Caroline was the daughter of John Hutchings, the Paddington spring-maker who had married Mary Daniels, Sidney's aunt. The marriage may have been arranged, or she may have been in the Daniels household at that time and he may have been keen to find himself a wife. His visit of over a year could have been sufficient for a brief courtship.

Sidney and Caroline married in 1903, following which they returned as planned to India to continue his service. Salaries for civil servants were good by local standards. In later years, as Indians were allowed to join the Civil Service at lower ranks, the British were paid ten times more. But the conditions would have been hard. Summers were hot and winter rainfall high. In 1907 they returned to Britain for a six-month period, returning in December 1907.

In 1908 Caroline died. During this summer there was a particularly bad drought in the region, the water supply to the village became infected and she contracted disease. Indeed, the village was so badly affected that most of the inhabitants died, and it was abandoned. A gravestone at the Daniels grave plot in Rodborough states that she was buried in Patephur, which I believe to be Fatephur Sikri, a town to the east of Lucknow in India, and it is likely that she is buried in the Christian burial ground on the southern boundaries of the town. It was not unusual for villages to be abandoned, the region was being intensively farmed following clearance and the effects on the status quo were significant.

Sidney continued to work, but was transferred to another station until December 1909, when he was granted leave on medical grounds, possibly suffering the loss of his wife, or himself from poor water. He was allowed a leave from December 1909 to November 1910 and returned to Britain. During this period, he took a vacation to Switzerland with his brother Harold, probably because the clear air was excellent for convalescence. At some stage during this period of leave he met Annie Fraser Dixon, a Yorkshire girl who was better known as Daisy. She was the daughter of a bank clerk in Halifax, born in 1880 to Thomas and Eliza. She was later to become his second wife.

In 1910 he returned to India. But in 1911 he again returned to Great Britain for 'leave on private, urgent affairs'. He married Annie.

Record of a voyage from Bombay 1919
A passenger ship record of the return journey aboard the SS Pigu.

He continued to be promoted and by 1915 had become Commissioner. He was now primarily involved with governance of Lucknow and Allahbad, two large cities, and was probably based in Lucknow.

Lucknow High Court and High Court Allahabad   Built in 1916,
Allahabad still has the biggest courtroom in India.

In 1915-16 he was President of a special tribunal and took the role of Legal Embracer to the Government from 1917-1921. The time was one of unrest in India and particularly so in the north-west of the United Provinces region. There were riots in Katarpur in 1918 and Meerut in 1924. In 1912 the Indian capital was moved from Calcutta to Delhi, and as Delhi grew in significance it was moved out of the United Provinces region nearby. The United Provinces were primarily the regions that comprised Oudh and Agra; the capital of Oudh was Lucknow, and the capital of the United Provinces was Allalabad.

During this time, he had several special appointments and senior acting positions before finally rising to the position of Puisne Judge in 1925. The role was that of the second most senior judge in the Province shared only with eight other judges, for the United Provinces, the largest region in India. In 1925, the Oudh Chief Court of Lucknow was established to replace the Oudh Judicial Commissioner's Court through the Oudh Civil Courts Act, something in which he will have been instrumental.

In October 1926, The Honourable Mr Justice Sidney Reginald Daniels I.C.S. retired and returned to live in Oxford, the city that he had come to know through his university period. His thirty-seven-year career had led him to the top in the Indian Judiciary, a long way from his engineering roots in Rodborough.

But he continued to be active in his retirement. In 1929 he contested the bye-election for Bath for the Liberals. He achieved 29% of the vote but lost to the Unionist Party. He stood for the same seat a few months later in the General election and increased his vote, but still came second. He stood again in 1931 and again in 1935, but the Conservative candidate was extremely successful and he lost share. Only achieving around 23% of the vote. He devoted a good deal of his time to the work of the Proportional Representation Society and was Chairman of the Executive Committee. The Society, started in 1884, had been inactive from 1888-1904, but in 1904 John Humphries became full time secretary until his death in 1946.

Their belief was that the voting system for MPs was not democratic and that a proportional representation system with one man, one vote for a truly democratic vote was the fairest system.

During the 1920s supporters included H.G. Wells, Bernard Shaw and Lord Birkenhead, a Conservative Lord Chancellor. Much work was done to devise fair voting systems, and although proportional representation was not adopted in Parliament, the Society became actively engaged running fair elections for trade unions, the Church of England for the Assembly, and numerous educational and professional organisations, like the General Dental Council, up until the Second World War. The organisation still exists and carries out work for governments and other organisations, to enable fair elections.

Sidney wrote a book covering some of his work entitled *The Case for Electoral Reform, with the Examination of the Principal Objections*. It was finished just before his death and published posthumously in 1938.

 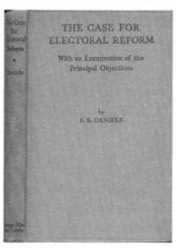

Sidney Reginald Daniels and his book on electoral reform.

By 1935 his health was failing. That winter, he and Daisy took a holiday to sunnier climes: to Palma, returning in March on the SS Pegu, the ship that had taken him to India so many times before. At the November 1935 election he failed to gain the seat in Bath and in 1937 he died. His wife continued to live for many more years at Boars Hill, Oxford.

Chapter 13. T.H. & J. Daniels – 20th Century.

Thomas Henry Daniels and Joseph Daniels

The T.H. & J. Daniels business was prospering. By 1888 they employed thirty-five men. Joseph's sons, John Stewart and Frederick Lionel, did not go to university but entered the business on leaving school at sixteen in 1888 and 1892. Joseph Harold started in 1898.

Thomas Henry Daniels, who had been the senior partner of the firm, died on 5th and was buried on 9th June 1897 in Stroud Cemetery, aged fifty-eight. He lived in Beaufort House, Stroud. As we have seen, he had been an ardent member of the Masonic Fraternity and, on the very day of his funeral, he was to have been invested as Provincial Grand Sword- Bearer of the Province, to honour twenty years dedicated work as a freemason. He had been a member of Stroud District Council, a staunch Conservative, and had for many years been a trustee of the Rodborough Endowed School, and a churchwarden for the parish. Thomas left no children. The executrix of his will was his wife, Elizabeth Martha Daniels.

Joseph was now in charge, and soon after Thomas Henry's death John took on the mantle of sales, whilst Frederickk Lionel learned more about running the manufacturing plant and the business side of the operation, and so the four continued to grow the business under Joseph's leadership through to the war.

Photograph of Daniels Foundry

Old Mill building used as store and workshops, to the left the first workshed.

It is no surprise that the three brothers were always keen to embrace any new technologies, and whilst photography was not new, having created excitement through the Victorian era with a stream of new developments, it was starting to be become a hobby for those who could afford the cameras and plates. John Stuart was a keen photographer and would visit places in the area to photograph views and record the buildings; a part of his collection is in the archives at Gloucester. In addition, he photographed people and did portraits of the family and friends. Harold was also keen and would also travel in the area, recording the flora and fauna.

Frederick taken 1902 and Harold

Their interest and pleasure is probably why from the turn of the century they started to create a record of the vast array of specialist machines that the company made and products that they had to sell. However, there was also a practical purpose to their archive, because it recorded the construction of the machines, to help with building further models, and the photographs could be used as a sales aid when describing the machines to potential customers. Although the brothers were photographers themselves and spent time at the weekends on the hobby, they also involved local photography firm Edwin C. Peckham, who, from starting his business in 1919 in Stroud, had an illustrious career for over forty years, possibly to develop the images and make prints.

We are fortunate that the archive of photographs still exists and we can draw on it, together with other documentation available. What it shows is a highly dynamic business that could turn its skills to any number of products in a variety of different industries. Whereas the business had been built on supplying local iron working parts for both the local mill industries, local construction and housing, it now moved in wider circles on bigger projects. The earliest photographs dated record a 'hairpin' machine and a mortar mill from 1898.

Another well-documented device was a gas plant. Gas was a popular fuel; its use had been widespread from the Victorian period, when gas plants had been developed to carry out the destructive distillation of coal to produce town gas. Most towns had plants that supplied gas to consumers for small-scale lighting and heating, but the provision was limited. Some companies were too far from the

64

mains supply, others required more power than could be supplied, and in any case it made more commercial sense to generate your own gas than to pay another company.

John Stuart is recorded in 1912 as an 'Engineer and Gas Plant Producer' and earlier in 1903 a 'Gas Producer' patent application had been applied for by John Stuart and Frederick Lionel to the Canadian Patent Authorities. The gas plant was a machine for burning a fossil fuel, such as wood or anthracite, and producing gas that could then be used to power a machine or generator.

Mills and factories were originally set up next to streams to utilise the water power to drive machines; however, this resulted in most businesses being in hilly areas and limited the locations of the machines. Factories now needed to be bigger to enable mass production, and good sites were becoming harder to find. Steam engines were an alternative, but they were cumbersome, taking space and with little control over their operation. There was no widespread use of an electricity grid until the middle of the 21st century, but electric motors were an ideal way of powering machinery: they could run an individual machine or a bank of machines, were easily switched on and off and were more compact, a big advantage, as space in factories was often an issue; but the electric supply was an issue. Later, the petrol engine was an option, but the fuel was volatile and relied on the machines to be well made to prevent accidental explosions, and many were not. The possibilities of fire in a factory were something to be avoided at all costs. Equipment to tackle fires was rudimentary to non-existent and the local fire service was reliant primarily on support from local businesses, and was very patchy across the country. In addition, their equipment was limited and often inadequate. A fire could destroy a factory and result in bankruptcy for the owner.

The Dudbridge Iron Works in nearby Dudbridge had a wide range of gas-powered generators and engines that they manufactured for local businesses, with a wide range of powers from 1HP to 30HP, and Daniels manufactured gas plants suitable for obtaining gas from coal. The generation equipment ranged in size: some of it was large, and the proximity of the manufacturing to the railway to enable the transport of finished equipment will have been invaluable. The size of the plant required depended on the application, but the Daniels site had a gas plant capable of 300HP for around 500 staff, and so 1HP would have met the needs of a couple of workers or a family home, while 30HP would have been adequate for a small factory.

We do not know if there was an agreement between the Dudbridge Ironworks and Daniels; however, the Dudbridge company was part- owned by Alfred Apperley and he probably will have had some influence over the two companies working together. For Daniels, the machines created a considerable income for the company through the early parts of the 20th century.

*50HP Gas Plant installed at A.C. Harrison 1890s; Gas Plant in 1905 with a T.H.
& J. plaque soon after the company was 'named'..*

Like many companies that had started as blacksmith's, it was natural that Daniels focused on providing a service to the local industry. Products were generally bespoke 'one-offs' to meet specific applications. The Gas Plant production provided an opportunity to start manufacturing in greater volumes, realising economies of scale in design and streamlining production. Occasionally in blacksmithing there had been a quantity of one item on order, and these would have been produced as a batch, but now, with the scale of the product, an area was set aside for a continuous flow of boiler manufacture.

Now, in addition, Daniels started to market their core products: they advertised in trade journals and took stands at national shows, including London and the Midlands. This product gave a higher profile to the business, provided them with more bespoke design for one-off products, but more importantly demonstrated that they were capable of providing volume production for companies that were becoming involved in mass production.

1911 Coke Suction Gas Plant; a Daniels exhibition stand featuring Gas Plant

Frederick with engineers driving a 1HP 'car' around the streets in Bristol, 1899

Mass production was in its infancy in the engineering sector in the early part of the 1900s. To a degree the Americans claim credit, with their implementation of the production line for the Model T Ford in 1908, bringing affordable cars to the masses, and earlier for implementation in machine tool industry. But it was perfectly possible that the scale of those industries have ensured that the events have been recorded, whereas the actions of the multiplicity of smaller companies have not.

Certainly the advent of the car industry brought new demands on the Daniels with orders for multiple items, some of which were manufactured in batches and others in continuous runs. Daniels supplied Harvey Frost & Co Ltd with Tyre Vulcanizers that they manufactured from 1900 until 1914. Harvey Frost, started in 1903 and based in Hertfordshire, survived for many years, specialising in vehicle manufacturing equipment and ultimately breakdown and repair truck equipment through until the 1970s. Tyre manufacture was to feature at Daniels for many years with Dunlop as major customers, and as tyre designs changed from solid rubber to pneumatic with treads, the need for machines to form and mould the tyres continued.

1900 Tyre Vulcanizer, Car trolley jack

The earliest records of Daniels manufacturing pumps date to 1909 with the type VI pump of which they made many for different companies, and we can only assume that they had manufactured types I to V over a number of the preceding years; certainly the designs by now were complex and well specified: a 1910 type VI pump for the Chloride Electrical Company was capable of 100 gallons an hour. At some later stage, Daniels worked with the Excelsior Engineering Company at Bowbridge on pump development, and manufactured their patent high-speed pump before developing a Daniels high-speed pump, which sold in volumes.

1909 Type VI pump; 1910 pump for Chloride Electrical Company; Sinking Pump

68

*46,000 gallons per hour pump for the National Transcontinental Railway,
Winnipeg, Canada; Sinking Pump (note the gas plant to the left of the shot);
Daniels manufactured Excelsior High Speed Pump.*

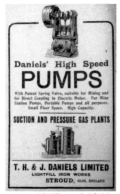
1917 and 1919 adverts for high-speed pumps and gas plants

The Daniels site had a further advantage in that it was large, capable of projects requiring space for casting large piece-parts or for mechanical construction trials prior to shipment. This resulted in a number of major projects, including many of the footbridges on the stations of the railway line now known as the Chiltern Line. Cable cars were also being constructed to enable people to ascend the mountains, and the company carried out the bespoke design and built the equipment on site prior to shipment.

Daniels constructing Saunderton Station Bridge in 1901; and in use today nr. High Wycombe, Buckinghamshire.

'Ropeways' for cable cars, 1901 and 1926.

River Boat Engine for a Paddle Steamer, 1911

70

In 1902 the first set of official accounts were produced; they showed the sales for the year were £6,230 from the Lightpill Iron Works and £4,251 from the CAM Board Mill. The company had six investors who had loaned money and a bank overdraft of £418; so the total owed was £4,600, leaving a net value of the company of £17,000. By today's money that's equivalent to over £1 million.

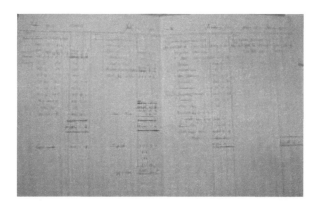

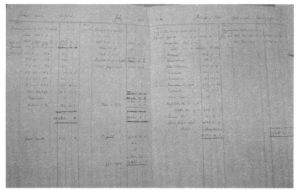

1901-2 Accounts

The name officially became T.H. & J. Daniels in 1904 when a law was passed requiring businesses to be registered as Limited Liability companies. T.H. & J. was the main company that had the Lightpill Iron Works and Daniels (CAM) within it. The company was registered with a capital of £25,000 and shareholders were Joseph, John Stewart, Frederickk Lionel, Clara Ada, and Joseph Harold, known as Harold. Also shareholders were E.P. Higgins, an engineer from Rooksmoor and P.G. Dewis, a traveller from Northampton. Harold, who had a particular skill with finance, became the secretary, a position he held until 1936 when he retired through ill health.

71

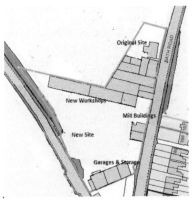

Plan of site after construction of new mill buildings in 1905.

The covered yard and the plate shop in 1902.

During the whole time of the company's existence, there was virtually a continuous building programme to meet the needs of the rapidly expanding manufacturing. Year on year there were more products and a wider variety of manufacturing techniques; they made ever- larger pieces; there were more designs and then they mass-produced them.

Originally they rented Fern Cottage and the area they used to set up the foundry. However, reference to the accounts tells us that Fern Cottage was purchased and the field that bordered the site was bought from Mr Jeffries. The extra space provided by the field was used to improve the water supply with the construction of a pond. It was dug into the hillside and may have relied on being filled from the water table, or there may have been a stream on the new field. The field was also used to continue the on-going building program.

In 1905 a new mill building was constructed on the land below the foundry for the increasing number of lathes and tools being used and to provide assembly space for boilers and machines.

In 1906 a new pattern store was built by Drew, the builder and brother of Ann Drew, who had married Frederick Lionel. In 1907 a riveting shed was constructed, in 1910 a new cart shed and in 1913 a garage. In 1916 a new machining bay was built that was quadrupled in size in 1918, and a 'women's facility' was built to support the war effort, for the first women in the factory.

Much of the materials used in the buildings were manufactured onsite, the steel framework was cast on-site as were the window frames and the steel cladding. Guttering, downpipes and doors were all made by the workmen, to designs produced by the Daniels designers. The relationship with Drews resulted in the use of brick: they were engaged in building using bricks manufactured at the nearby brickworks.

The 1905 Mill Building and the 1918 building.

73

The foundry

The building extension under construction 1920

Roof structure of the 1905 Mill building whose other end has a wooden roof structure, the only wooden roof on site, probably constructed in the 1918 War when steel supplies were prioritised for the war effort.

The metalworking shop around 1900

Casting ironwork, 1936

The 'Garage', which was originally open- sided. Note the original iron cladding made on-site.

Factory units built in the 1920s viewed from the extension built in the 1940s. Iron parts were made on-site including cladding, extraction, staircase and iron windows for light to allow machining and fine work.

The large 1940s workshop today showing the roof construction of greater span and the cranes for moving heavy presses and machines.

The early workshops were open and had few windows, but in time the importance of lighting was recognised. However, Daniels were progressive and the later factory was designed by Mr Thomas Falconer a renowned local architect famed for his arts & crafts designs. It had large windows, top lights and clerestory windows. Clerestory windows were unheard of in an industrial building and it was done to provide maximum light and give a huge feeling of space and airiness. The windows were precisely located to light the work bench areas. The casement windows, a key feature of Arts and Crafts, were designed by Mr Falconer and were amongst the first in the area, made on site, they were a blueprint for his windows in other arts & crafts building and opened another market to Daniels. The building was precisely located in the correct direction so that there were no shadows and to maximise light through daylight hours. There were no obtrusive pillars, the walls were seemingly wafer thin with large glass areas, but there were included enormous overhead gantry cranes built into the design that could lift products onto the higher mezzanine level. The factory was of great length, the steelwork centre structure being of huge strength but was virtually un-noticeable. The design could, and indeed was lengthened easily. The design was ground breaking. So proud were the family and workforce of the factory that it was here that was chosen as a location for works photographs.

Thomas Falconers' son Peter also became an architect of global standing. He is mainly known for two things, the first is the remodelling of High Grove House for Prince Charles, and the second was that he had a reputation for Industrial Buildings and is known for creating 'Big Box' Industrial buildings that revolutionised the designs dramatically increasing useable volume by 20%, using techniques from the Daniels building gained years earlier.

The company also had sufficient funds to pay the Government land tax, a single payment that enabled no further taxes to be payable on land owned, saving money in the long run and making the land more valuable.

But the company did not just invest in the site; it invested in houses. In 1904 Hill View Cottage was purchased, then in 1913 Rose Villa was purchased, Frome Terrace in 1918, Field View in 1919, Rose Place in 1920 and No1 Clarence Villas in 1926. It's likely that some of these properties were also built by Drews. In 1928 the factory, land and properties were valued at £11,700, whilst the business by then had an asset value of £17,600.

Some of the architectural design is ornate, was it again the hand of Thomas Falconer.

Hill View, Rose Villa and No1 Clarence Villas on Bath Road opposite the works.

Part of Frome Terrace

These houses were put to good use for the business, which was expanding rapidly and needed skilled workers that had to be either trained or attracted to the business from another area. The issue of housing was certainly acute through the First World War and so the provision of housing was imperative. As an example (jumping ahead to the Second World War), a clever young, university-trained mathematician and engineer, Jan Stiassny, arrived in 1938 from Czecoslovakia; he was the son of a Jewish family and was escaping the Nazi holocaust. His skills were ideal, but he needed accommodation to enable him to work at the factory, so he stayed with Mr H. Guest, who was living in the company house, Rose Villa, letting rooms to staff of the company. The arrangement was ideal for T.H. & J.. Jan was fortunate to have escaped. The British Government had only just started to allow Jews to come to England, but the Germans then stopped them leaving. Jan's sister missed out on receiving a permit to leave by one day too late, and was murdered in the gas chambers along with his parents.

He started work in the drawing office but went on to become an engineer, and married a schoolteacher, Lynn. They bought the cottage in the grounds of Whitecroft, the house that had been owned by the Daniels. Much later in the 1960s, when I was a boy, Jan taught me how to play chess and introduced me to stamp collecting.

Mr Guest was still living in Rose Villa in 1947, paying a rent of £21 per year. He later moved to a house near Whitecroft.

78

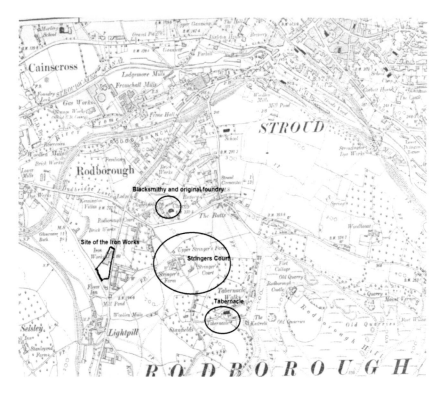

1903 Map of Rodborough showing the Blacksmithy, Iron Works, Stringers Court and Tabernacle.

MARRIAGES.

DANIELS—DREW—On May 3, at the Wesleyan Chapel, Chalford, by the Rev. W. R. Garlyon, of Stroud, assisted by the Rev. S. Whittaker, of Brimscombe, Frederick Lionel Daniels, third son of Joseph Daniels, of Lightpill, Stroud, to Ann Winifred Mary Drew, eldest daughter of William Farinton Drew, of Chalford, Stroud.

Gloucester Citizen May 5th 1904

Marriage of Frederick Lionel and Ann Winifred, taken by John Stewart.

But we have jumped too far ahead. Frederick Lionel married Ann Winifred Mary Drew on 3 May 1904 at the Chalford Methodist Church, which had been built by her grandfather. She was the daughter of William Farinton Drew, a Civil Engineer, and Building and Engineering Contractor.

The Drew family, William Farinton front left.

The Drews were a family of builders; in 1903 the family business, the Drew Brothers, William, George and Thomas Henry, had been dissolved, allowing them to go their own ways. In addition to her father and grandfather being builders, her brother also was in the profession.

It is likely that it was through the churches that Frederick and Ann met; Ann was deeply interested in church work and a singer of repute: from an early age she would often travel to other local churches and chapels to sing. She was a pianist and joined with other family members as an orchestra to visit chapels to play where they had no organ. Frederick was a member of Rodborough Tabernacle. The organ was not built until 1932, and so it is likely that she will have sung and played at his church. After they married, she became active in Rodborough Tabernacle: she ran the Sunday School for many years; she sang in the choir and was heavily involved in the Home Churches Fund, of which for many years she was honorary secretary.

A clock presented to Frederick and Ann by the Daniels staff on their marriage (Stroud Museum; their first house in Coronation Road.

Frederick and Ann moved to their first house in Coronation Road in Rodborough. It was a new build and Ann's father probably built it for them, possibly as part of a wedding present. The house was on a larger plot than those around, looked out over fields and was not built next to for many years. In 1905 she gave birth to Frederick William, known as Eric and in 1907 Joseph Lionel Daniels, known as Lionel. In addition, Ann and Frederick had Beatrice, Elizabeth, Kathleen and Barbara. John Stewart had no children and so these were the next generation destined for the Daniels business.

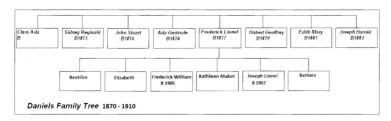

Daniels Family Tree 1870 - 1910

Family group with Elizabeth, Kathleen, Beatrice & Barbara; Ladies outing by horse & cart from Stringers Court ~1920.

The Daniels-Drew relationship became sealed with the building of some of the buildings on the Daniels site. Their construction was of a steel framework with corrugated iron cladding. Daniels designed the buildings and manufactured the parts, whilst Drew carried out the construction. This construction technique was not new to Daniels, and part of their business was to build factories for other businesses: in 1897 they had drawn up plans for a factory to manufacture boracic acid for the Boron Products Company. The project was for a new company to be formed on the existing site in Inchbrook; the extension to the factory was estimated to be £16,000 to build and was a huge project for Daniels. By 1901 the project had floundered: the mine in Asia for production of the raw material for production had still not been purchased and the company's plans had changed. As a result, Daniels sued the Boron Products Company for the design work that had been put into the project, a total cost of £240.

On 27 January 1919, William Farinton Drew, Ann's father died. In his will he left £5,065, a considerable amount, split between his son and Frederick Lionel Daniels. A married woman at this time would not have had her own money, which explains why it passed to Ann's husband, but it is unusual that anything would have been inherited as it would normally pass to the first son; this probably indicates how close the families were, the will intended to seal the building and steel work manufacturing alliance.

Daniels manufactured Trusty Oil Engines from 1899 and in 1916 Daniels bought the Trusty Engine business from Frederick Avens and Co., a Cheltenham based company after the business ceased trading, and produced the engines until 1934.

1905 Trusty Oil Engine

Chapter 14. The First World War

At the start of World War I in 1914 the importance of the engineering sector was not fully appreciated by the Government. Before the war many engineering businesses, fearing its onset, had started to lay off workers to counter a recession. In addition, there was opportunity for workers to join the army to fight. There were no employment contracts, many workers were lowly paid and many simply stopped turning up for work. Government orders for munitions and equipment were slow to be released partly because it was believed the war would be short and no new supplies would be needed. In the event, the British Army ran out of munitions and it was only through luck that at the same time the Germans did too.

Britain failed to develop an early plan in response to the outbreak of war. Debates arose between 'Navalists', who advocated the use of naval power to create blockades to Germany, and 'Continentalists', who advocated a military approach. Winston Churchill believed the nation could maintain a business-as-usual approach and the consensus was that the war would last no more than nine months. However, by the end of 1914 a maze of 475 miles of trenches stretched from the Swiss border to the North Sea. The situation required vast supplies of rifles, machine guns and ammunition. The strategy of trench warfare required offensive support from large volumes of high explosive shells, but by the end of 1914 supplies were exhausted, and British batteries were rationed to firing six rounds per day. Both sides were suffering in the same way and it allowed the trenches to be greater developed and more impenetrable.

The Government, becoming aware that the supply chain for ammunition was pitifully limited, and realising the problems they were in, looked to Industry to help. The large artillery shells and cartridges were made on lathes, and Alfred Herbert was the largest lathe and machine tool manufacturer in the country. He was also chairman of the Machine Tool Association, and, fearing Government intervention, had written to Lloyd George assuring him of the industry's full support for Government orders. Alfred's help was enlisted by the War Office. He was able to identify the companies to whom he had sold lathes and thus who was capable of manufacturing the shells. He was taken on by the Ministry and given a special role to sort out the supply problems; this he did by increasing the manufacturing capacity, placing orders on the companies, who could then ramp up production and would then place orders on his business for more lathes.

However, the biggest initial problem was lack of manpower. Some of the companies had lost up to 50% of their workforce to the war effort, although to a great extent it depended on employment relations as well as local sentiment about the war. And so Alfred was instrumental in a law passed by Lloyd George which allowed women to work in factories and stopped men leaving unless they had express permission from the company in which they worked.

Prior to this, women had not been officially allowed to work in factories, although more unscrupulous employees had turned a blind eye when there had been pressures for workers, and women had worked as subcontractors and in small home businesses.

However, although the laws were passed, it was not always clear on how the law should be applied. Within the engineering sector, much work was subcontracted from the bigger companies to subcontractors. These were initially included on the list of companies which were off-limits to military recruiters, but were later removed because it was difficult to identify whether they were working on military contracts or not. In the midlands for example, the fifty firms initially identified were reduced to seven by March 1915. A survey of machine tool companies found that 74% of companies had lost between 10% and 29% of the workforce, 14% of companies losing over 30%.

The introduction of women into the workforce was also proving problematic. Alfred's company was pioneering and had already pre-empted the Government's edict by introducing 'trainee girls' in October 1914, but the tasks that they were carrying out tended to be menial support activities rather than hands-on engineering, although it did tend to free up skilled engineers. There was a general reluctance from the male-dominated workforces of companies; women were paid less and the jobs were highly skilled, pay scales being determined nationally. As a result, there were several companies that experienced strikes: with a tight labour market, unions had more power and the potential for conflict was increased. Increases in overtime and the introduction of night shifts helped alleviate the situation, but with a ninety-hour week as common practice, with reports of men working up to 132-hour weeks, or more. In March 1915, Lang & Co were reported to have 800 men working 'night and day' to meet special government work. By the end of February 1915 over 10,000 engineers were on strike in Glasgow, and local wage negotiations were able to pacify the situation.

There were also practical issues with the arrival of women and unskilled labour in the factories: firstly training – it takes time and manpower to train someone; this resulted in a short-term loss of output. Many of the machines being used for production were general and of great complexity, not ideally suited to the task of munitions. The engineers argued that quality would drop; however, the Government was committed to quantity.

The demand for tools was immense and soon outstripped supply, resulting in other companies entering the marketplace to make lathes. The majority of the lathes were required for standard shells, and as such, the Americans were ideally suited to help supply, with their ranges of standard machines. But there was a great need for new machines.

The situation was compounded by demand for ammunition and weaponry from France to supply their troops where they had lost some factories to the war and the supply chain from German manufacturers ceased. The situation was further aggravated because the bullets and shells were different from the British which resulted in a new range of machines being needed. This was repeated with the Russian Army and it soon became clear that British manufacturing was becoming the manufacturer for Europe. In addition new weaponry was being developed, a wide range of aircraft were being developed across the country for military use.

However, the 'Shell Crisis' continued and Lloyd George now formed the Ministry of Munnitions in a direct attempt to resolve the issue. By 1915 there was a political crisis and the Liberal Government was seen to have failed with its initial, amateurish approach to the war, being replaced by a War Coalition under Asquith. While British engineering had dramatically ramped-up production to support the war, the response was seen as piecemeal and inadequate. The Ministry of Munitions now assumed control of the major manufacturers in order to co-ordinate activities.

Alfred Herbert had good relations with his staff and was able to lead the way in the employment of women, and, through the Machine Tool Association, encouraged others to do likewise; by September 1918 24.4% of those employed in the machine tool trade were women.

Percentage of total females employed in Machine Tool Trade

Month	Percentage
January 1916	2.5
September 1916	9.0
January 1917	10.7
September	24.4

T.H. & J. Daniels used Herbert lathes and so a connection between Alfred Herbert and the Daniels was made that was to continue for many years. It is unlikely that Daniels had lost many of the workforce to the war, and so was able to react to the increasing orders placed upon the business, the introduction of women being seen only as a way of keeping up with demand. Relations with the workforce were good and the Daniels family were progressive in their outlook. By 1915 there were over forty women working in the factory. We have photographic evidence that they were not just employed on menial activities but were operating lathes alongside the men. These skills will have taken time to learn and we can probably surmise that they started in the factory on munitions soon after the onset of the war.

The introduction of women, however, brought its own problems. For instance there were no suitable women's toilets or canteen facilities. There was no experience of managing female staff and space was already at a premium.

86

There were additional problems in the manufacture of shells requiring explosives: the factory was based around a foundry, space was limited and the risks of explosion were great.

Daniels' solution was to build new toilets and facilities, which they located directly over the pond that was used as the water source for the factory. This saved on using valuable land space and provided a cover to the pond, to reduce the risk of water poisoning from the enemy. Next to the pond they dug into the hillside to create a cave that was used to store the ammunition; a steel grate was put in place so that the explosives and finished shells could be kept under lock and key. The advantage to storage underground was that in the event of enemy bombing, the factory would not explode.

In reality, the Stroud valley was reasonably safe and an excellent place to manufacture armaments; indeed it was a useful facility for all sorts of wartime development.

On 29 Nov 1915, a photograph was taken of the factory workers on day shift. It also shows Joseph in the centre, flanked by Frederick (left), Harold in front and John Stuart (right). In front of John Stuart are E.P. Higgins, Vic Hodges, P. Rodway, Cecil Hall and Lionel Day.

Photograph of the day shift during the War.

In addition, Ann started at the factory to manage the women who had been taken on, around eighty women by now in total. As a result, she was to become more involved with the running of the business, and joined the Board, a position she held for many years.

Daniels' engineering prowess was noted within the Government, probably by Alfred Herbert, as there was a great synergy between the two businesses, and other contracts from other departments followed. At one stage, the entire output of

87

the factory was focused on supplying contracts for every government department including the War Office, the Ministry of Supply, the Admiralty and the Air Ministry. As well as producing ammunitions, the factory produced hundreds of 'limber wagons', material for mine sweeping, engine parts for submarines and a variety of experimental projects for War Office and the Admiralty. So important was the site that it was refused a licence to do any work for other customers.

Photographs taken to mark the first women in the factory, working a shell on a lathe and assembling the shells.

Photograph showing the women working alongside the men in the construction of munitions.

Capacity at the factory was limited by space. The ammunition had to be kept well away from the foundry and in the secure area, which was deep inside the buildings. The machine shop was extended, but materials were hard to come by, as was the labour. Extensions were built. The roof structure was of wood because of the shortage of metal. In addition, the lathes were at capacity, and so to alleviate the problem a night shift was started so that manufacturing ran twenty-four hours a day. In 1918 a photograph was taken of the night shift.

1918 Night Shift, Machine Shop.

The war effort was a success and the company had gained a lot of expertise both technically and in learning new manufacturing techniques.

A de-poisoning lorry developed during the war to clean water supplies poisoned by the Germans. It is unknown if it was ever used.

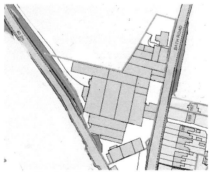
Factory layout around 1918.

89

Towards the end of the war in 1918 Frederick Lionel Daniels bought Stringers Court, Stringers Farm and estate lands from Sir Alfred Apperley. This provided him with the space required for his growing family, further land for expansion of the business and access to new water supplies that were vital for the factory. The area was not built up and from his house he could walk across his fields to the factory. John Edward remained at Briarton Villas and John Stuart at Fern Cottage. But the history of Daniels' connections with Stringers goes back further, as Joseph's nephew, George, had been a tenant at Stringers Court much earlier.

Collecting in the harvest on Stringers Farm.

During the war farm labour was difficult, and so workers from the factory were dispatched to help out. It was vital that the farm was made to be as productive as possible, as food was in short supply. A couple of photographs from 1918 show the girls collecting corn, including Miss Sally Mills (2nd from right) who was to become P.G. Rodway's wife.

View of Stringers Court and a group haymaking around 1920.

Chapter 15. After the War

When the war finished, orders from Government Departments ceased. The factory was left with nothing to do. Prior to the war the company had an extensive network of sales agents both in the UK and through the Colonies. By 1918 all the work was going elsewhere and Daniels had no agents at all. They had to start again seeking out work for the factory, building the network of agents. In some areas, development in Britain had been left behind and they identified companies that had patented products in other countries but had yet to introduce them into the UK. They did deals to obtain British rights and then set about manufacturing them for the home market. This included centrifuges and water softeners that were important for the company over the following years.

In addition there were new developments. An electrical grid was conceived and, under the auspices of local electricity boards, it was constructed. Daniels manufactured parts, insulators were formed from Bakelite using Daniels presses, Daniels centrifuges were used to separate oils that were required to make transformers and other iron and steel parts were made. Daniels were also on the board of the local Electricity Company.

Bakelite was invented in 1907, it had started to be used as an insulator during the war, but its full usefulness became appreciated during the 20's and 30's and it remained a major material into the 50's. Using a press that applied heat it could be moulded to create a rigid plastic for many application, telephone casings, kitchen utensils, electrical insulators, radios and later TV's.

Clara Ada and Joseph continued to live at Fern Cottage until they died: she died in 1919 and he in 1921. Joseph left the business in fine shape with well-equipped modern workshops and a healthy business. John Stewart took on the role of managing the business with Frederick Lionel by his side.

Harold bought Whitecroft, a large house with on the road to Nailsworth. He remained single but developed an interest in nature and would often go out exploring the local area's flora and fauna, using his camera to record his findings. John Stuart was also a keen photographer and combined this with his interest in china and glass.

By 1918 they had designed parts and had a collection of 5,000 pattens; by 1935 this had increased to 9,500. They were involved in engines; they had bought the Trusty Engine business to provide their own motors for the gas plant they produced, and continued development of this engine through the 1920s. The range of products was wide, including manufacturing water softeners, cranes, rag chopper and rag washer equipment, air and water pumps. They designed all the equipment they used at Daniels CAM for leather board manufacture and supplied other businesses in leather board and paper manufacture.

Patten Book

Machines they designed included a pin- making machine, a varnish stirrer, a pneumatic gun, a buffing machine, an eyeglass frame- bending machine, a tennis racket machine, a golf ball press and bottle caper.

In 1922 Daniels exhibited at the Wembley Exhibition with a stud feed saw bench that was made to half-size just for exhibition purposes.

Half-size stud feed saw bench for show purposes

Around half the customers were outside Gloucestershire and orders from abroad included the East Indian Railway and a company in Winnipeg in Canada.

In 1924 they received the first order from James Gordon for turbine brackets; the relationship was to end in Daniels buying the business many years later. In 1925 Daniels designed their first centrifuge, a market that they were also to be involved with for many years.

Turbine blades used in a high-speed pump for water.

In 1926 they had the contract from the Stroudwater Navigation Co. for swing-bridges along the canal in Stroud. Many remained until recently, when the canal has undergone extensive repair. The Lodgemore Mill Swing Bridge was built in 1928 and remained intact until 2016 when it was replaced.

The works plates survived on both outer girders; however, they were in a sorry state of repair. During the removal, one plate was handed to the Cotswold Canals Trust and CCT member John Ferris suggested it could be restored by his friend, Arthur Keenan.

Nick Rieger, who owns Ryeford Engineering at Cainscross and who served his Daniels apprenticeship between 1970 and 1975, supported Arthur in what was a complex re-assembly and welding task to restore the sign to its original condition. The repaired cast iron nameplate now occupies pride of place on display inside the Cotswold Canals Trust Visitor Centre at Wallbridge Upper Lock.

The T.H. & J. Daniels sign returned to its original condition.

93

The Lodgemore Mill Swing Bridge, photographed in 1928, across the Stroudwater Canal in Dudbridge, was built to replace an earlier wooden swing bridge in c.1928. Re-photographed in 2016, prior to its replacement.

The bridge under construction in the factory.

The year 1928 also saw the introduction of a press designed as a tablet-making machine for pressing medicines into tablet form and the first hydraulic press. Within the next couple of years they had designed 50-ton, 75-ton, 120-ton, 250-ton, 600-ton and 660-ton presses. The investment was significant but the demand for the equipment was growing. Presses were relevant to a wide range of applications and introduced the rubber industry to the Daniels. Customers included Avon Rubber Works at Bristol, Reliance Rubber and Dunlop. In addition, Daniels had a range of tyre- testing equipment.

Presses were developed from the screw press to the powered.

Gramophone presses and a power- driven press.

Other large customers of Daniels included Filmophone, for whom they produced an escutcheon for a radiogram in 1931, and the Cathode Corporation in Barnet, who were supplied with a cylinder for a vacuum chamber used for manufacturing either valves or cathode ray tubes. In 1932 Daniels produced a high-speed agitator for Sharples, and started another relationship which was to end in a takeover.

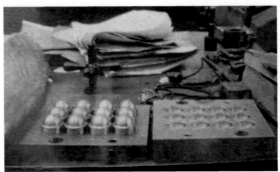

Golf balls manufactured in a press

Daniels were also working in other materials in addition to iron, steel and copper; they provided parts in aluminium, including engine parts for the Air Ministry, phosphor bronze and nickel alloy.

In 1927 Frederick Lionel of Stringers was listed as a Land Tax Commissioner. The Land Tax was introduced by the Government in 1693 to help pay for the war with France. The tax was managed and collected locally by Commissioners, who were appointed by local MPs and had to have an income from land of £100 per year and be gentry or professionals, such as doctors and 'pillars of society'; the role was unpaid. The first Bill resulted in the registration and tax levels for the property with a second Bill in 1798 providing more control and including an option to redeem the tax for a lump sum of fifteen years' tax, so that no more tax was payable. The Daniels had paid the tax on their own lands and so had no vested interest in the tax, but by taking on the role, they will have been able to work for the common good of the local people, reducing taxes where possible and ensuring a fair hand with its implementation. In addition, it re-enforced their position in society. The tax was finally abolished in 1963.

By the late 1920s the economic conditions were difficult: the Government after the war had decided that the country was to return to the Gold Standard, where printed money was backed up by gold reserves. They had abandoned the connection during the war and printed money to finance the war effort, but now the return resulted in continued deflation of the economy. The German economy had not recovered from the war and relied on foreign loans, which came mostly from the US. The American economy had been buoyant but was overproducing goods for the home market and sales from overseas were not forthcoming As a result, there was a stock market crash in October 1929, following which the economy declined, banks collapsed, savers withdrew their money, mortgages were foreclosed and businesses closed. This in turn led to the collapse of the system set up to handle international loans, and resulted in Germany's not being able to pay for imports, resulting in a fall of international trade. Commodity prices fell by 45% over a three-year period. Then the US Government compounded the problem by imposing an import tariff on goods of between 40-50%; the rest of the world followed suit and it resulted in a crippling of trade. Britain suffered along with the rest of the world and by 1930 unemployment was 20% with 2.5m out of work.

The Daniels business suffered along with others. Most businesses laid off their workers; however, the Daniels decided they did not want to lose their skilled men and found other work for them. One time they deployed the workers to resolve the water supply for the site by digging a new reservoir and water system.

Water was an issue for any manufacturing plant. In the early days, water was pumped up from the well and a reservoir created above the site to provide running water throughout the site. In time this was insufficient and so water was pumped from the river below; however, this water was reliant on goodwill and the water levels in the river. One major reason they had bought Stringers Court was that it had the springs for the supply of water to the factory. Stringers Farm had an important source of water, and years before they had bought a house above the Bath Road, enabling them to divert water under the roadway to increase the supply.

A larger reservoir had been created on site, but space was limited and so it had been built over during the war to provide toilet and rest facilities required for the influx of women workers. This also had the added advantage of protecting the supply from a feared poison attack from the Germans.

But in summer the water supply from the springs above the factory was not adequate, and in winter there was risk of flooding. The solution now was to build a much larger reservoir above the site. This ultimately increased the ability for water storage and over the following years more land was acquired with springs that were diverted into the storage system, until virtually the entire hill side water supply was channelled down into the site. The reservoir became so large that in later years the boy scouts used it for boating.

The on-site storage was increased to accommodate more water. The system served the site well through the following 50years. The only problem was a major flooding incident in the 1980's when the tank capacities proved inadequate and the factory was flooded. The system pre-dates planning and it was discovered much later when a developer was building a new development above the site and discovered the enormous pipes that lay underground to channel the water. The overall size of the ponds is unknown but water was an essential requirement for heavy manufacturing.-

Also other building projects were undertaken on the factory when there was a shortage of work. In addition, there was an increased emphasis on farming activities at Stringers where men could be used to grow and harvest crops. The farm stretched from Stringers to the road up Walkley Hill and it was decided to sell the plots of land along the road for building houses, thus raising more funds.

But the reduced pressures on production enabled an increase of focus on new developments; this was fuelled by the arrival of the next generation of Daniels, who, brimming with enthusiasm and full of new ideas; arrived at the business to start another new cycle within the company.

Frederick William and Joseph Lionel went to Wycliffe College before going on to university. In 1924 Lionel went to Birmingham,, where he studied Engineering. One of his additional interests was in religion, fuelled by the family connection with the Tabernacle, and he joined the Christian Union. There he met Marjorie Helen Mills, who was studying to be a Doctor.

Helen, born in Birmingham in 1903, lived in Acocks Green, a couple of miles from the University. She came from a working class family and had been brought up in the Church of England. Her father was a Sporting Gun Action Maker in the gun trade and her mother a schoolmistress. For a girl to be studying medicine at university in the 1920s was extremely rare; what makes it even more unusual is that she worked part-time to pay for her tuition and other living expenses.

She developed an innate sense of caring for people, and during her time at university, she would go to the poor areas of Birmingham to administer care for the sick and dying. She graduated in 1927 and went to Nottingham, an area of great poverty, to find work, knocking on the doors of doctors until she found someone to take her into his practice. She worked in Nottingham for a while, continuing to help the poor, visiting the slums in her spare time when she was not in general practice. This was the time before the National Health Service: life was tough, the economy was suffering, work was in short supply and the poor could not afford medicines, and so she treated them and provided medicines for free.

Lionel continued his studies at Edinburgh University and served an apprenticeship at a company in Wales, but would travel to see Helen when he could. They continued to share their common interest in religion and at some time travelled to America to a conference of Congregationalists. She must have found the Daniels family and business set-up daunting, coming from her own small family. Her father, involved in the gun trade, one of Birmingham's oldest technical trades and the country's largest manufacturing region for guns, will have recounted stories of manufacture on lathes and machines of intricate parts; coming from Birmingham, the great industrial force in the Industrial Revolution, she will have known something of business. However, it will still have been a challenge to get used to such a close, dynamic family with a major business within a country town. However, she eventually agreed to Lionel's proposal of marriage.

Chapter 16. Rodborough Tabernacle

Skip back to the 1500s and a small minority of people were starting to question the religious teachings from the Catholics in Rome and the newly formed Church of England by Henry VIII. They banded together, discussing alternatives and looking at reforming ideas that would improve the lives of the proletariat. By the 16th century they were better organized and became known as the Puritan movement. They were looking for a freedom to worship, and wanted an alternative to the instructional teaching laid down by the Church of England.

The most famous Puritans are the Pilgrim Fathers who sailed the Mayflower to America in search of better times. They laid down the foundation stones of religion and democracy for the USA. Many of them came from North Nottinghamshire and Lincolnshire, where there was a strong Puritan movement, and where later the Wesleys were to create the Methodist Church.

By the mid-17th century there were many factional, puritanical groups like Baptists and Independents in addition to the Church of England, which itself had factions with widespread beliefs and practice. Reformers were trying to change the church from within with philosophical debate on the necessity of bishops and the hierarchical structure.

In 1660, after the restoration of the monarchy, Charles II decided to exert his authority through the Church: he brought in a series of draconian new laws instructing on worship, together called the Clarendon Code. The hierarchy of bishops was restored and clergy of the Church of England were required by the Act of Uniformity of 1662 to conform. Over a fifth did not and, as a result, they were ejected, thrown out of their churches. Many took part or the whole of their congregations with them, although this was difficult because all who persisted in worship that did not conform to the new Book of Common Prayer were 'nonconformist', and were barred from holding any meeting of more than five unrelated persons, from holding public office and were liable to persecution, including imprisonment, the confiscation of their property and the destruction of their meeting houses. They were also compelled to pay tithes to support the clergy of the Church of England.

In 1689 the Act of Toleration ended the worst of the persecution and permitted the licensing of places of worship for many nonconformists, but not all. But it paved the way for the growth of the Congregational churches, which provided a platform for some great inspirational leaders, passionate about religion and with it social and political reform.

George Whitefield was born in Gloucester in 1714, the son of a publican; he was fortunate to receive an education enabling him to go on to Oxford University, where he was to meet John and Charles Wesley. He was from a poor family, receiving a scholarship to cover fees and had to work his way through university, acting as a servant to other students. He returned to Gloucester, where he was ordained by the Bishop of Gloucester. He then preached locally and in London, adopting the practice of preaching in the open. His following grew and in 1738 he decided to go to Georgia in America. Whilst there he saw a need for a children's orphanage and in 1739 returned to Gloucestershire to raise funds.

On Sunday, 1 July 1739, George Whitefield preached on a Neolithic long barrow, now known as 'Whitefield's Tump', on Minchinhampton Common above Stroud. A young man called Thomas Adams was in the crowd and was so impressed by Whitefield's preaching that he gave the land to build a Tabernacle as an independent Non-Conformist place of worship. The building, the Rodborough Tabernacle is today as it was, built of local stone and opened in 1749. It grew to become an important place of worship for the area.

In 1740, after some huge open-air rallies in the UK, George returned to Georgia and set about building the Bethesda Orphanage. Continuing his evangelical work, he travelled across America preaching every day to crowds of thousands. In the UK, the Wesleys took over where George had stopped, and continued to preach in Gloucestershire as they did throughout England, forming the Methodist Church.

But Rodborough Tabernacle was run more along the lines of George's beliefs than the Methodists, and followed Calvanistic principles, becoming known by the 19th century as a Congregationalist Church, which primarily means that the running of the church was up to the congregation. There was no hierarchy of bishops, archbishops, priests, government or a pope to define doctrine, but a simple belief in Christianity and the Bible. The church was run by two deacons, who were elected members of the congregation, and it was they who organized the services and booked the preachers and clergy to take services and organized for their payment.

Rodborough Tabernacle was free to follow its own path of religious discovery, and in the early days there were many great preachers who travelled the country raising issues and ideas from the Bible, but relating them to the modern world. The Church did not fight the onset of science and technology in the way the Catholic and established churches did, there was no hierarchy to be feared by the people and change was embraced when it was needed. Indeed, the Church helped their congregation in every aspect of life, including business, because it was through business that wealth could be created. That would then be used for the good of the people, both through the Church and through other means.

The Free Churches, the largest of which were Wesleyans and Methodists, were strong throughout England. Birmingham in the Victorian era had twice as many chapels as churches with seats for 30% of the population, although most people did not attend church regularly. The situation was replicated in many other big cities, like Liverpool and Leeds. Most officers in local government were practising Christians, but the proportion of Free Church members was much greater.

It is unknown how long ago the Daniels family became involved in the Free Church, but the Daniels acquired the land on Bath Road to build their first factory from the Tabernacle sometime around the 1860s and were heavily involved at this stage in the church, a relationship that was to continue for the next 100 years. The Tabernacle helped them to grow the business whilst probably receiving some funds for the land, which could be used to grow the Church. It is interesting to note that in 1871 all the pews were made for the church, a not insignificant expense. In the 1860s Alfred Apperly was also a parishioner; he, Joseph and Thomas Henry will have been encouraged to work together for the common good, resulting in the desire to serve in office for the good of the people, through schools, councils, hospitals and other organisations.

The ideas that the people could manage their own affairs and were responsible for each other lay at the heart of the prosperity within the Stroud Valleys through the Victorian era and into the 20th century. It was the responsibility of those in positions of wealth and power (which usually went together) to ensure the prosperity and welfare of others. Today we know of these ideas as "empowerment".

The Rodborough Tabernacle also led to the creation of other Free Churches in the local vicinity, all with the same dynamism to support business and industry for the sake of the common good of the people and the congregation. The environment was one of enthusiasm and confidence: if George Whitefield, a lowly son of a publican, could go to Oxford, and travel America building his Church, then anything was possible. As a result of these beliefs and through seeing others achieve great things, many entrepreneurs created great businesses from unique ideas in the Valleys. Members of the Daniels family became lay preachers; themselves from humble origins, they could attest to the opportunities afforded to Congregationalists through the Free Church and encourage the risk taking needed in business.

But there were other fundamental differences between the Free Church, the Catholic Church and Church of England. The ability of a Church to adapt to scientific ideas is reflected in an issue of basic theology: a simple example of the difference between the Churches is the sacrament. The Catholic Church says that the wine given at sacrament is the blood of Christ and that to be a true Catholic this must be believed; this is still the case today. The Church of England also says that it is the case; however, it accepts that it is difficult to justify and subject to discussion. Congregationalists believe it is symbolic. Scientifically, it cannot be the case and for the Daniels as engineers and later for Helen Daniels, as a doctor, this was more believable, and was one of the issues that allowed Helen to convert from her Church of England beliefs to the Congregational movement, and she became a staunch active supporter throughout her life.

The Tabernacle influenced the development of the Daniels and the people of Stroud in its thinking. The Daniels followed these Christian preachings, and over a long period of time the Daniels were on committees to help oversee the management of the parish councils, town councils, hospitals, schools, water works, museums, cemeteries, freemasons, Rotary, local Scouts, District Scouts, engineering institutions and of course, the Church.

All the work was unpaid, and often the Daniels business provided charitable donations, but they saw it as their duty. They were not unique in these beliefs as there were many others with wealth and influence, who also worked alongside them, working for the better good of Stroud and its people.

In 1902 the Government passed an Education Act that included in it the mandatory teaching of Christianity. In addition, a new tax was imposed that would pay for the education. The Church of England was the beneficiary; they already had their own schools and a hierarchy that had a greater connection with the Government than other independent church organisations. This allowed them to introduce their Christian doctrine into all schools. Philosophically, the Church of England was a structured and controlling organisation, whilst the Free Churches advocated power for the people. The law was unpopular; although now most people agree that the desire for a good basic education helped the country progress, it acted to marginalise other churches and religions. Untruths could be spread, such as the myths about alcohol. The Free Church believed in moderation in all things, including alcoholic consumption and preached on the evils of drink. This was translated as a ban on all drink by the Church of England and was ridiculed in its teachings.

Joseph Daniels objected, along with many, to the Act. He refused to pay the tax, or that part that provided funding to the Church of England. As a result, in August 1903, as a 'Passive Resister', he was taken to court in Nailsworth for failure to pay, along with Rev. S.J. Ford, Baptist Minister for Minchinhampton, Rev. C.S. Davis, Baptist Minister for Stroud, Enoch Knee, George Garraway, Charles Clark and Albert Philpott. The court was crowded and there was cheering in support of them until the magistrates threatened to clear the courtroom of the audience. The Resisters argued that they had right on religious grounds for the tax to be reduced. The Rev. C. A. Davis had paid the tax to the value of £4 8s 6d, refusing to pay just one penny in the pound, or 4d. They were told that whilst their objection had been heard, the court was not empowered to determine the rights and wrongs, only to apply the law of the land. The gentlemen all paid their dues.

But Joseph had joined the Rodborough School Board in 1902 and shortly after joined the Stroud Education Committee, together with other prominent Congregationalists to ensure, amongst other things, an unbiased treatment of Christian teaching in the local schools.

Rev. C.E. Watson

Charles Ernest Watson, A.T.S., was born at Cleethorpes on October 28, 1869. He was brought up in the Church of England, but became a convinced Congregationalist: he held to the end of his life a very clear spiritual ideal of the fellowship of the church. This ideal was at the base of all his pastoral work. He was trained at Lancashire College under Caleb Scott, and obtained the diploma of the Senatus Academicus. His first pastorate was at Lymm, 1898-1903, and from there he went to Oakhill, 1903-09. In 1909 he entered on his long pastorate of thirty-three years, 1909-42, at Rodborough Tabernacle, Gloucestershire.

At Rodborough Mr Watson did his life's work, beloved by a faithful and loyal people and by his young folk, who rallied round him and were one of the great joys of his ministry. In 1921 he was Chairman of the Gloucester and Hereford Union, and from 1917-1935 the Secretary of the Gloucester and Cheltenham district of that Union. He was also for many years the Free Church representative on the Gloucestershire County Council Education Committee. In the Stroud Valley he held, at one time and another, every position of honour which the Free Churches could confer upon him. His name will long be remembered in Gloucestershire; and on the Cotswolds he is likely to become a tradition as "Watson of Rodborough". His pastorate at the Tabernacle was one of very high distinction.

Mr Watson was great as a friend, and his personality had a wonderful charm. He was a man of very wide culture and of the most varied interests. He had a sound knowledge of liturgiology and was also a trained archaeologist. His *Rodborough Bede Book* is one of the best service books of recent years. But all these interests were only by the way; his real work was the ministry, and he died literally worn out in the service of Christ. He passed away on 1 August 1942, and was buried in the Tabernacle burial ground. The funeral service was conducted by the Revd Robert Nott, of Ebley, and the Revd Alan Beesley, the assistant minister at the Tabernacle and now Mr Watson's successor in the pastorate.

Chapter 17. The Years 1930 to 1950

TH & J Daniels 1931

At 6.30 am each morning the horn would sound out across the valley and could be clearly heard across Stroud, where most of the workers lived. It was the Daniels' morning call. The next, at 7.30am, was sounded at the start of work, by which time all had arrived for the long day ahead. Breakfast was served in the early morning break in the works canteen, thus ensuring a well-nourished workforce for the rigours of the day ahead.

For most the work was hard. The foundry was hot and the air thick with smoke and dust. Some of the work was heavy, with large gantry cranes for the biggest parts. Men crawled into the steam boilers under construction whilst red-hot rivets were inserted and then hammered into place by the men outside as well as in. The noise was tremendous and the risk of deafness was high. The electric arc welder was developed between the Wars and introduced to improve the jointing of metals, but riveting was preferred on many projects where metal expansions varied and welds would have been subjected to undue stresses. The welding was blindingly bright.

In the workshops, the motor-driven lathes continuously droned whilst the rows of men, and, during wartime, ladies, worked on making piece parts to high degrees of accuracy. There was a huge energy about the plant as parts were moved from area to area, into the assembly shops, to the test bays, then onto packing and shipping.

The factory site was far from level, so the moves entailed a continuous flow up and down the site; heavy parts were difficult to manoeuvre and it was often hard work with boilers over three metres in diameter and twice as long. As in all industrial plants, accidents happened. In September 1895 John Butcher was injured when a flywheel flew off a machine and fractured his thigh and knee; he was taken to Stroud Hospital, which, in the days before the NHS, was funded by local companies and charitable support. T.H. & J. were donating about £2,000 a year in charitable donations to the hospital by the 1930s. There is rumour of a death at the plant, but no evidence other than the story of the death whilst digging out the well.

The raw materials of pig iron, coal, coke foundry, steel bars and plates also needed to be moved in from the railway on delivery, the railway now being the principal mode of transport replacing the earlier canals.

The inadequacy of electricity as a source of power was typical to most businesses; the widespread use of electricity in business and in the home did not come about until the 1960s. Gas generators were more popular because petrol was more dangerous; however, later Daniels acquired a motor manufacturer that increased their capability to offer a wide variety of gas, diesel and petrol-driven generators for use in industry throughout the valleys and the rest of the country.

The work at Daniels Cam was also messy: the floor was deep in a soggy slush created by the leather pulp, which smelt vile. In later times, paper and card were introduced as a constituent, eventually replacing leather, but the slush on the floors continued for many years. This was early recycling, paper and card were collected from every source and later used to make fibreboard for the back of radio and TV sets and to stiffen suitcases.

The Daniels family always spoke fondly of their workers, particularly the skilled staff, without whom the business would not have been a success.

After university, Lionel went on to Edinburgh to work at an Engineering Department gaining experience, but whilst he was there he received a Telegram informing him that his father had been taken ill. He re-assembled his car, which was in bits, and drove home.

What he found was that the business was suffering with only 3 days being worked every fortnight and there were 135 men on the books. So he called on 24 different companies a week until the orders started to arrive, and he turned the company around.

Lionel brought with him new ideas from his time in his studies and from his observations of manufacturing in industrialised Birmingham. His education had opened his eyes to the world outside of Gloucestershire, and for many at the works, who had lived their lives in the vicinity and dedicated their careers to the company from apprentice to management, he was alien.

In 1932 Lionel and Helen were married in Warwickshire. Frederick, ever grateful to his father in law's marriage gift of a house built for him and his bride, gave a similar gift to the newlyweds. He owned Stringers Farm and had land that extended to the road up Rodborough Hill and along the Bath Road opposite the factory. He was selling off some of the land, in part to help stave off the recession that was deeply affecting the country, to enable houses to be built, and he gave a plot for a bungalow, Innisfree, to the young couple.

Innesfree on Walkeley Hill. A candid family photograph.

Their first son, John, was born in 1933, followed by David, Peter, Philip and Ruth. John, David, Peter and Philip continued the family tradition of attending Wycliffe College.

By 1935 Lionel and Helen needed more space for their growing family; his income had risen as he had taken on more responsibility in the factory, and so they moved to Overden in Nailsworth, leaving the bungalow to be acquired by T.H. & J. as a further property within the portfolio.

Eric had started a few years ahead at the factory, but he was not as technically minded and didn't have Lionel's knowledge of engineering. At some point the factory at Cam suffered a fire and Eric was dispatched to sort out the problems, which he did. However he stayed to run the board factory leaving Lionel a greater role at the main site.

Lionel, meanwhile, was fast learning and got on well with the workers on the shop floor. As he gained more orders it was natural for him to see them progress through the factory and it was not long before he knew exactly what was happening on the shop floor and in all the Departments.

Lionel's father and uncles had grown up together, brought up in a modest cottage on site, where they had learned about the craft and always been around the workers. They had played together and been together at school when it had been small, taking part in activities together. The brothers had entered the business together, working as a close-knit team under Joseph's guidance for over twenty years; they had their personal strengths and weaknesses and worked to complement one another. But the next generation brought succession issues: historically, when life expectancy was short, wealth was passed onto the first born son, but John Stuart had no children, so the succession would be to Frederick's sons, but Eric had no eye for business. He had been bought up in a large, remote house and had been to a school with children from a wealthy background, where he had enjoyed the fun aspects of all the extra-curricular activities. He did not inherit the drive and passion to create wealth and indeed had little comprehension of monetary worth. Lionel, however, was in total contrast: intelligent, well-focused and an all-round individual. However, the sons did not get on together. The sensible solution was therefore that Eric would be given Daniels CAM as an autonomous business to run, a challenge that was much smaller and that he was thought capable of, while Lionel would continue to be employed in the main works. Ultimately, if Eric proved himself, he could then move to take up the reins in the main business – but this was unlikely.

But John Stuart remained at the helm as Chairman for most of his life. Harold died in 1936 and Frederick semi-retired to work on interests in the wider community. He was an outgoing man who enjoyed meeting people; he enjoyed committees and being at the centre of decision-making. It became clear that life within the confines of Daniels was too narrow and he took up more positions of responsibility as we see later. Lionel was not treated as 'special'; John was in charge and surrounded himself with his own management, and Frederick could not be seen to give any privileges to his son. John Stuart also had other interests, one of which was Masonry and he encouraged his senior staff to become active members of the fraternity, giving time off freely for them to attend meetings. This acted to bond the management team into a stronger clique that Lionel was not a part of. In fact, he later maintained that he disliked Masonry because of the time it took away from the company, but for him it was divisive and he grew to dislike the organization, whilst he was also aware that the times were changing in Britain and it did not have the value to the company that it once had.

Socialism was on the rise, a fact that had been subject of debate at school and his university. Birmingham was the first to have a Students Union. There were risks associated with the old order. Masonry was associated with gentrification and business, both of which were becoming social enemies. In addition, the Daniels business was now much bigger than the locality, and it was insufficient to spend time in such a closeted environment as local Lodges and Committees. Local government was being radically centralised, schools, hospitals, water and power all coming under national control. He knew change within Daniels was necessary, but for most of his working career it was not in his power, and so he worked hard for the benefit of the company, whilst always maintaining the feeling of an outsider with the Managers.

Lionel was a quiet, thoughtful man who was at his best in one-to-one conversation. Meetings did not suit him and he felt frustrated at the time lost to them. When he finally did take control of the overall business in the 1950s he was in his forties, and was so used to operating to side-step the management, communicating directly with those carrying out the work and getting things done, that changing the management was not a key priority for him. Cyril Dyer was Works Manager and also another Wycliffian and Lionel had great respect and a great rapport with him. It was through his direct contact with him and his other 'hands-on' managers that Lionel ran the business.

Eric, however, never really fully rose to the challenge of managing Daniels CAM, leaving it in the capable hands of his deputy, whilst he enjoyed his main interest that he had acquired as a boy at school, Scouts. By the 1940's inheritance taxes were over 50% and despite not paying themselves huge amounts, choosing rather to re-invest in the business; the Daniels' personal wealth in properties had grown on the back of inflation, and so Eric, who was the eldest brother and least capable of looking after himself, inherited enough for himself and his sister for the rest of their lives, whilst Lionel inherited shares in the business.

A gathering of staff visiting Grimshaw Hall, near Birmingham 1930.

Eric did not marry but continued to live at Stringers Court with his parents until their deaths, together with his sister Elizabeth, known as Betty. She suffered mildly from Downs Syndrome, before it was recognized as such, and was unable to look

108

after herself. He continued to look after her in the family home, even after his parents' death, until he died. Ironically, she outlived the rest of her generation.

Gramophone Presses, 1931; Milk bottle filling machine 1930.

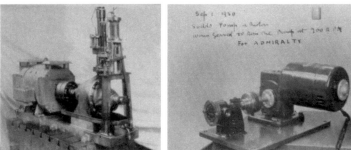

Pump for HMS Neptune 1935, a light cruiser built in 1933, which was sunk off the coast of Tripoli in 1941; Pump for the Admiralty 1938.

Two of many Rotoplunge pumps manufactured for Lever Bros at Unilever; Lister engine-driven Rotoplunge pump for the Pyrene Co Ltd. 1940.

Pumps assembled.

Daniels had been doing some work on and off over a number of years for a company called Erinoid who manufactured a type of plastic. The company was never very involved with Erinoid and always felt they deserved more, but it probably resulted in the business becoming more involved in the plastics industry with a range of tools for working and pressing newly developed plastics.

Exhibition Stands in the 1930s.

In 1933 and 1934 Daniels filed a number of patents, some of which were involved with injection moulding of thermoplastic material such as cellulose acetate.

This work led to Daniels becoming a leading expert in the business of plastic moulding and forming; an area of expertise that they held through until the 1960s. Alfred Herbert recognized the importance of the developments in plastics and the world-leading technical skills within Daniels and in the late 1930s Daniels started a business relationship with Alfred whereby Daniels products were sold by Alfred. In time the relationship went further as the plastics industry developed.

Latex spooling machine; Dunlop tyre testing machine

How much this new sphere of development was influenced by Lionel is unknown, but he was aware of the research being carried out in Britain, was always keen to see new ideas in the trade press and was involved in the Plastics Institute from its early days.

In 1937 the company exhibited at the British Industries Fair with plant for synthetic resin moulding, pumps, accumulators, presses, valves, hobbing presses, preforming machines, preheating ovens, steam, electric or gas platens, injection presses and structural steelwork.

Lorry in the factory loading with centrifuges; Representatives receiving 'Sharples' centrifuges on behalf of a Chinese Government agency.

We can see a progression with new machines; the business was embracing new materials, one of which was rubber, a product literally growing on trees in Malaya, a part of the British Colony. Moulds and presses were being built that could form

111

these into products with great intricacy and accuracy. Products from tyres to washers to gloves could be formed.

The company also developed a supercharger for aircraft designed by Captain Eyson, although little is known about this.

Nowadays, it is generally accepted that the best toy in the world is Lego, but it was pre-dated by mini-brix, small rubber bricks preformed to fit together that could be used by children to build buildings. These were made with Daniels presses and act as a great example of how the development of plastics required the development of moulding and pressing machines to create the Lego that we know today.

Fan units and dust extraction ducting used for dust extraction.

Manufactured 1942 for Pratt Daniel Ltd., Large scale dust extraction unit and fan blades used within a fan unit.

The largest single casting, a 6 ton machine reinforced baseplate produced in 1950s and the factory location where it was cast. Consideration had to be given in design to crane capacity.

The factory used as a foundry in the 1930s and as it is today (2013).

Foundry with girders in production and the furnace, around 1930.

Construction of the new machine shop roof.

There are more common examples existing of the work from this period; the most common around Stroud are road drains.

Road Drains made by T.H. & J. Daniels

Chapter 18. Plastics

The first man-made plastic was created by Alexander Parkes, who publicly demonstrated it at the 1862 Great International Exhibition in London. The material, called Parkesine, was an organic material derived from cellulose that, once heated, could be moulded, and retained its shape when cooled. After cellulose nitrate, formaldehyde was the next product to advance the technology of plastic. Around 1897, efforts to manufacture white chalkboards led to casein plastics (milk protein mixed with formaldehyde). Galalith and Erinoid are two early trade name examples. This was the forerunner of Bakelite, a material that also had electrical insulative properties and became widely used in the introduction of electricity, used in switches as an insulator.

The Erinoid factory was started in 1913 in old mills the other side of the road from Daniels in Lightpill. Originally, the company had been located in Middlesex, but relocated. Alfred Apperley's son had relocated to Middlesex, and Alfred was instrumental in investing in a number of businesses and relocating the companies to Stroud.

It was the only factory outside Germany that produced the material that was used to make a wide range of products. Chemicals were added to cows' milk that was brought in from Ireland; dyes were added to provide the required material colour, then the liquid had to be poured into a mould, which would dry as a solid block or it could be pressed into the required shape, using a mechanical press. The blocks could then be milled or worked to form the object required.

The original machines used on the site were imported from Germany, where the originator for the process using dried milk powder had lived before moving to Stroud. But the War will have stopped any further import of machines, and it is likely Daniels will have been involved to some degree, considering their proximity, capabilities and friendship with the Apperleys. In later years, Daniels were heavily involved in plastics and the processes, so it is reasonable to suppose that this came about through Erinoid. Originally, mixing was carried out in small quantities by hand, but eventually larger- scale production was required and Daniels became involved in the development of machines for mixing chemicals, machines that would ultimately be required over the forthcoming years for the development of the larger scale plastics industries. In addition, Daniels developed presses to form the materials into objects that were then sold.

The material was marketed as a non-inflammable substitute for many things: celluloid, bone, amber, ebonite, horn, coral, fibre, ivory, jet, vulcanite, tortoiseshell, turquoise. It was ideal for turning and admirably suitable for making electrical fittings and accessories, buttons, beads, combs and hair ornaments, cigarette holders; knife handles, pencils and penholders, hatpins, umbrella and stick handles, organ stops, and piano keys.

Charles Rennie Mackintosh, the designer and architect, became interested in the material in the early days of manufacture and used it decoratively on furniture. It could be shaped and moulded and made in a wide variety of colours, ideal for an entrepreneurial designer. His lead was followed and from then on it was incorporated into many items of everyday life.

By 1914 Erinoid employed 125 people and made five tons of Erinoid a week; by 1933 this had grown to 500 people. Throughout this time they had machines and parts made by Daniels and some of the buildings were constructed using their steels and steel sheeting.

Machines for Erinoid 1936 and 1940, including a Hobbing Press

The 1947 British Industries Fair advert lists the company as a manufacturer of modern plastics materials: casein, cellulose acetate, vinyl plastics, polystyrene and oil-soluble synthetic resins.

Buttons and a sample sheet for handles; a drawing of the original site

By 1973, 700 people were employed in the Erinoid factory. Additional products included polystyrene as well as other thermoplastics, but by the 1980s the market was becoming too competitive and the company closed.

However, the involvement of Daniels with Erinoid opened up new market opportunities. Between 1908 and the 1950s a wide range of different plastics with different characteristics were invented. T.H. & J. were at the forefront of development of industrial plant for their application and worked with many companies, large and small, on some leading research. In addition, they did research of their own and through the 1950s were carrying out work that they patented, primarily related to injection moulding of the newer plastics. T.H. & J. were ideally positioned, having knowledge of plastics and processes for plastics manufacture, a range of hydraulic presses, expertise in fluid dynamics from high-speed pump design and expertise in tool design. Daniels products became instrumental in the growth of the plastics industry in the UK as more applications were identified for the new materials.

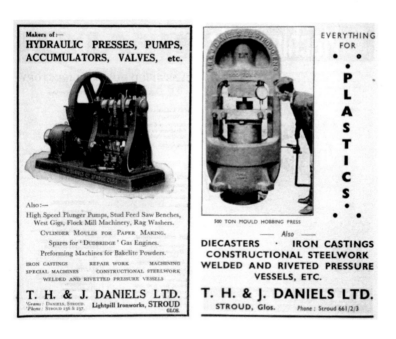

Adverts from 1936 & 1943. The small boy is likely to have been John Arnold Daniels.

Chapter 19 World War II

Joseph Harold died on 10 February 1937. He never married, remaining in Joseph's cottage for many years before eventually buying Whitecroft, a large house in Nailsworth. On his death, his estate was worth around £29,000, of which he bequeathed £500 to Stroud Hospital, £1,000 to Harold Redston, Secretary at T.H. & J., and £500 to Percy Rodway, Engineer. These were large sums: £1,000 was well over two years' salary. In addition, he gave £500 to his godson, Daniel Nourse Downes Watkins, £100 to his cousin Harry Holmes Isacke, £500 to Rosa Stella Isacke, Kate Hamilton Isacke and Muriel Isacke and £500 to Edgar Harold Meize. The residue of his property went to John Stuart and Frederickk Lionel. John moved to Whitecroft until his death, following which the house was used as the Head Office for Pratt Daniel before being sold, sadly demolished, and the land used for building houses. The Daniels retained some of the land for many years; it was used for growing Christmas trees before that was also eventually sold.

Joseph had married in 1931 and originally lived at Innesfree, a small bungalow on Walkeley Hill. It was built in the grounds of Stringers' Court which was owned by Frederick Daniels. The land had been sold to a developer who built the houses alongside it. The sale of the land was used to expand the factory, with the purchase of additional land and new larger factories erected. Later, Joseph moved to Overden near Nailsworth; the bungalow was kept as a worker's house until Joseph's son, John, and his wife moved into it when they first married. What is interesting is that they paid rent to the company – everyone had to pay their way! Frederick remained at Stringers Court whilst John Stuart lived at Whitecroft.

By 1940, both Joseph Lionel and Frederick had become Directors of the business. The facility was again turned over to supply for the war effort. By 1942 the number of men employed rose from 310 to 400 whilst ninety-seven women were employed where before there had been none. A Government survey of all businesses was carried out and concluded that this was the maximum capacity of the factory with the maximum labour available limited by housing in the area. The company had around sixty permanent members of staff, or salaried staff, with the remainder as more temporary workers, on wages. Section Managers earned £5 a week, skilled workers around £4; in the drawing office and on the shop floor it depended on experience and varied between £1 and £4 a week.

A few of the men enlisted and went off to war, but the factory was important and skilled men were needed to stay and produce war supplies. Overtime was required in the factory to keep pace with war orders and a survey carried out by the Government concluded that the factory was at capacity. It was not possible to bring in any more staff, even if they had been available. Overtime was initially in the Drawing Office, but eventually it was required throughout the factory as more output was demanded. The hours were already long, so additional hours were hard for workers, but they were paid.

Overtime was approved to start on 1 March 1940: middlemen 5 shillings, girls and juniors 2/6 and 5% for managers. In October 1940 a Major J. O. Affleck joined the company, engaged for Works Defence. His salary was £5 a week, which was more than most; the management were earning between £3 and £6, technical staff between £2 and £4, with the majority of the rest less than £3, so the overtime was extremely helpful even if it meant longer hours on top of the forty-eight-hour standard week, with Sunday working as well. In addition, there was a Christmas bonus. Frederick Lionel earned £10 a week. £1 in 1940 would be worth about £40 today. Wages did not increase during the war, but income tax was increased significantly to pay for the war, and in August 1941 National Health Insurance was introduced to pay for the hospitals. In addition, there was inflation, rising by 10% in 1940 alone. However, there were fewer goods to buy in the shops, rationing was introduced, and the Government stopped the manufacture of many luxury goods like perfume, so what little money that was earned was adequate. Some of the men, such as Mr Burgess-Short went to war, though not many because of the importance of the work, and the wives of those who left continued to receive an income. Later, H.C. Dyer, L. Smith and M. Clutterbuck received an allowance for being in HM Forces.

The 1946 salary bill was just over £37,000: £17,000 on the general workforce for stores, repairs and superintendence and the remainder on management, administration, engineering and sales. In addition, the direct productive wage bill was £58,000.

The company carried out contracts for the War Office, but also had some top-secret work for Woolwich Arsenal, work that was to carry on throughout the war and for some time afterwards.

By 1942, the first multiple rocket launch system known as a 'mattress launcher' was developed by the Allies and was designed to be deployed on tanks and warships and landing craft, and were fired in support of troops in a landing action. The rockets were five-inch cordite sticks and the launching system, was capable of projecting a salvo of 800 to 1,000 rockets 3,000 yards (2.7 km) in around forty-five seconds. The weapon was also known as the 'stickleback', and it is this name that was used in the factory during its manufacture. It is likely that it was designed at the factory by staff, along with other military hardware and may account for Major Affleck's role in the business. They were used extensively in the D-Day landings.

In addition the factory made other tank parts, parts for Bailey bridges, shell casings, chainsaws for the MOD, tripods for gun emplacements and a 'special section' was set up for aircraft components. The section was to make parts for a new, top secret plane engine.

119

Sticklebacks in the factory 1943 and the Mark II version 1944.

Dr H.L. Guy, Air Commodore Whittle, P.S. Fowler (Vice Chair), J.S. Daniels (Chair), A.B. Cooper, Prof Andrew Robertson (President). The Western Section of the Institute of Mechanical Engineering Institute.

The jet engine, invented by Frank Whittle, was first used in a Gloster Meteor jet fighter. The plane, developed by Gloster Aircraft, was top-secret and not produced at their site, but assembled at a company in Cheltenham. How much was manufactured by Daniels is unclear; however, it is quite likely that the company was heavily involved and the decision to use Gloster Aircraft could have been as a result of the proximity to Daniels. At the time, local people reported seeing planes flying that had no propellers. These reports were generally ignored as ridiculous!

A part for Frank Whittle's jet engine on the shop floor, Dec 1943.

Barbara Daniels, sister of Lionel and Eric, had started in the business in 1940, but decided to help the war effort elsewhere, and joined the WRAF. She returned to the factory in 1946 but tragically took her own life in 1947. It was blamed on a religious sect that she had joined. Beatrice Daniels also worked at the factory until 1937 before marrying Alfred Hitchon.

Beatrice Daniels with Winifred at Stringers Court.

1924 Map showing growth of the factories on the site.

In 1946, just after the war, the biggest customer was Alfred Herbert with orders for injection moulding equipment; in total three machines were built in the year. A company called Sharples, who sold centrifuges, accounted for 25% of the company's output, while other companies included Gordons, Permutit and Dawson.

Permutit was a long-established supplier of water softeners. Based in London, their primary market was in the hard water areas around London. Manufacturing was subcontracted to Daniels who were heavily involved in the design aspects too, and by the 1930s they had supplied 10,000 units to domestic customers.

Advert for Permutit softeners and softeners; in the factory, 1928.

After the war, new machine shops were built further up the site to house new equipment. Offices were built with more Drawing Office space and for design engineers. The process of design and development was becoming more complex and the machines built were more technically challenging. The large coal and steam machines of the Victorian age had given way to petrol-driven motors that were becoming increasingly compact as the twentieth century progressed. In addition, the introduction of electricity countrywide provided an alternative power source to the water wheels for the machines used in the local mills, enabling newer, faster machines to be developed.

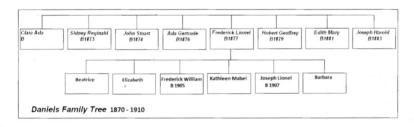

Clara Ada B	Sidney Reginald B1873	John Stuart B1874	Ada Gertrude B1876	Frederick Lionel B1877	Hubert Geoffrey B1879	Edith Mary B1881	Joseph Harold B1883
	Beatrice	Elizabeth	Frederick William B 1905	Kathleen Mabel	Joseph Lionel B 1907	Barbara	

Daniels Family Tree 1870 - 1910

Photograph about 1940 with (standing) Joseph Lionel, Frederickk Lionel, Frederickk William, (seated) Majorie Helen, John Arnold, John Stewart, David Lionel and Agnes Winifred.

In 1946 a Centenary Dinner was held at the Lilly Brook Hotel, Cheltenham. It was six years late, postponed because of the war. John Stuart, in his role as joint Managing Director, gave a speech reminiscing over his fifty-eight years, the longest- standing member of T.H. & J. Daniels. By now Lionel was Joint Managing Director and Eric was controlling Daniels (CAM). Also present were the fifth generation Daniels, John Arnold and David Lionel, of whom there were expectations that they would come into the family business.

The Daniels company did not forget the factory floor in their celebrations. A whole day excursion was arranged. The paddle steamer based in Bristol was hired, all the workers going under the Avon suspension bridge and along the coast to Ilfracombe.

Centenary celebrations at the Lillybrook Hotel.

John Stuart, Winifred Ann and Frederickk Lionel. Group photograph with Lionel, David, John Arnold, Barbara, John Stuart & Winifred, Beatrice?

In 1949 Frederick Lionel died (see later chapter), followed in November 1952, by John Stuart. John was well known in Stroud, President of the Choral Society and on many local committees, and throughout the West Country, through engineering connections, having held Presidential roles in three Engineering Institutes, working tirelessly on engineering projects. He was also an active Mason, Past Master of Hicks Beech Lodge, founder member of the St Lawrence Lodge and of the Stroud Lodge of Master Masons and member of the York Lodge. He was past Grand Deacon of the Grand Lodge of England and also Deputy Provincial Grand Master of the Mark Masons Lodge of the Province of Gloucestershire and Herefordshire. In addition, he sat on many other local committees, including Stroud Museum, and had an interest in glass manufacture. His hobby was collecting fine glass and china, including Meissen and he was keen on preservation. He and Harold were present at the archaeological study of the Woodchester Glass House which was a Huguenot glassworks. The 'dig' was carried out over a period between 1890 and 1920 by good friend and fellow industrialist Mr Basil Marmot with both John Stuart

125

and Harold involved to varying degrees, however nothing was recorded.. John Stuart was extremely keen on preservation and historical study and Daniels were involved in the organisation of the Cowle Museum from the late 1920's, indeed John was Chair at the start of the War and ensured the safety of the collection by moving it to a location of safety. In 1950 John, still Chair of the Museum that was later to become the Stroud Museum, was sole survivor of the 'dig' and recorded the work in a book.

The book written about the Woodchester Glass House and his original notes now in Gloucester archives.

Harold and Frederick in 1949.

John Stewart in Masonic regalia,1945; Winifred Ann Daniels

Joseph Lionel and Marjorie Helen

Chapter 20. Wycliffe College

There has been a close relationship between the Daniels and Wycliffe College from the school's inception, and it is therefore of no surprise that the influence from the school on the Daniels was considerable.

Wycliffe was started by G.W. Sibly in 1882 when the school at which he was teaching, Taunton, decided that he was not to take up the position of Headmaster after his father, Thomas, retired. G.W. as he was known was a popular and gifted teacher and the decision by the school board was unexpected to most, except, it seemed, G.W. He had already decided that, had he not been offered the headship, he would start his own school, and Stonehouse, being served by three main railway lines, would be a good place for it.

Not that this would have been a surprise, since his grandmother, who had been thrown out by her father when she had converted to Methodism, had started her own school in Plymouth and married the Reverend Nicolas Sibly, a Methodist preacher. Their fourth son Thomas, G.W.'s father, was the first headmaster of Queens College, Taunton, in 1843, and was acclaimed as a pioneer in education, believing that boys should be well fed, was opposed to corporal punishment, and that there should be a broad education alongside the classical subjects that were more commonly studied. And so, for G.W., teaching, Methodism and modernism ran in the blood.

The day after the decision by the board, G.W. travelled to Stonehouse to look at Haywardsfield Hall, which he bought, and converted the stables to schoolrooms for 100 boys. His confidence was immeasurable considering that the country was in recessionary times, and nationally school numbers were declining, and he invested his life savings and more into the venture. But his reputation was sound and in addition to the half-dozen boys and two masters from Taunton, who moved to join him, numbers swelled to twenty-seven boarders and four day boys from the first year. The name 'Wycliffe' was chosen because G.W. apparently regarded John Wycliffe as possessing many qualities, including 'independence, a sturdy Protestant attitude towards life and a pioneering spirit'. The school motto was 'Bold and Loyal', in English and not the traditional Latin.

The school ethos suited Joseph and Clara Daniels. They were forward thinkers, believed in education, and wanted the best for their children. Clara, as well as a good mother, was a gifted teacher and had given them a good basic education, whilst Joseph, who was calm, patient and a good communicator had taught them about business. And so when it came to secondary education, Wycliffe was a sensible choice.

Sidney started in the first year the school started and did well. He excelled at English and had inherited his mother's natural aptitude for languages, for Clara had a reputation in Stroud as the best French linguist in the area. He left five years later, having obtained a first class in the Cambridge Junior and Senior Honours examination. In the days before 'O' Levels, 'A' Levels and GCSE, the pupils took the Cambridge Junior Honours Examinations, the equivalent of GCSEs, and those who did well could continue to the Senior Examinations.

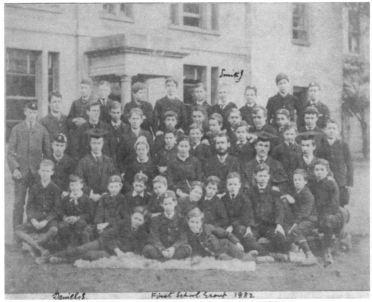
Wycliffe's 1st school photograph 1892

He went on to take the London University Matriculation exam, which was the standard exam for entry into universities and most higher learning institutes, remembering that there were not many universities at the time; most have been built since. It was run by London University. He achieved honours and took second place in the list, an incredible achievement for him and Wycliffe School, in its early years. But he was not alone and Wycliffe had many other boys who achieved success. He was offered a place at Oxford University and was awarded the Boden Sanskrit Scholarship.

The position of Boden Professor of Sanskrit at Oxford was established in 1832 with money bequeathed to the university by Lieutenant Colonel Joseph Boden, a retired soldier in the service of the East India Company. He wished the University to establish a Sanskrit professorship to assist in the conversion of the people of British

129

India to Christianity, and his bequest was also used to fund scholarships in Sanskrlt at Oxford.

At Oxford Sidney studied Law as well as Sanskrit and Hindi, and in the 1893 final examination for the Indian Civil Service (ICS) he was awarded prizes in Hindi and Law and placed top of the list. He continued his studies and trained for a career in the Indian Civil Service before leaving to take up his first post in India. The position of Boden Professor at Oxford University still exists today.

As an aside, in 1875 the Boden Professor at the time, Sir Monier Williams, established a fund to create an Indian Institute with Library and Museum in Oxford. In addition to the furthering of research into Indian language and law, the premises were to be used for the training the Indian Civil Service by the India office of the British Government. Much of the fundraising came from India, as it was seen that an Institute for the study of India would be useful: it would raise the profile of India in the learned centre of Oxford and create a place for Indian nationals in Oxford.

Indian Institute, Oxford

Built in the 1880s in two parts, it was located in the heart of Oxford on Catte Street opposite the Bodleian Library. Over the years it was expanded to include a library and museum of artifacts brought back by Sir Williams. The library was amalgamated into the Bodleian. In 1928 the University Governing Body took a controversial step by evicting the Institute from the building and giving the building to the History Faculty which specialized in European history. It created uproar, particularly amongst the families of the original donors from India as a fraudulent action and culminated in a formal protest from the India Government. The University Union accused the Governing Body of racism and the debate was heated. With some, the move by the University still remains a raw issue almost ninety years later.

In 2012 the James Martin Institute moved into the building, a centre for research activity funded in large part by James Martin, a private benefactor who made his wealth through book sales. His books, produced over many years, made predictions of the future, and he foresaw the Internet and other major breakthroughs before they became reality. More recently he died and the name has now been changed to the Oxford Martin School.

Returning to the Daniels in the 19th century: John Stewart started at Wycliffe the year after Sidney, followed by Frederick and Harold over the next few years. They lived in Stonehouse with their aunts, which was convenient and cost-effective. The arrangement gave   an income for looking after them and allowed Joseph to focus his efforts on his business during term time when they were at school. Joseph and Clara led frugal lives; any profits from the business were re-invested back into creating more growth through land, buildings and other investments. So it was fortunate that, with four sons to educate, Wycliffe was, by comparison with others, not expensive.

The school grew quickly both in numbers and expansion of buildings; by the second term there were forty-four boys and by the end of the year, fifty-nine. Many private schools set up at the time were the product of wealthy benefactors and had funding to support growth, and so what G.W. achieved purely with the income from boys, small loans from his father and goodwill from those around him was remarkable. It was even more remarkable how rounded the curriculum was, even in the first year. It encompassed all manner of modern and forward-thinking subjects, a Literary Society that Sidney particularly enjoyed, which debated such subjects as the abolition of the House of Lords, the Disestablishment of the Church, capital punishment and the inadequacy of the Armed Forces, a Reading Society and a Field Club that captured the imaginations of John Stewart and Harold with talks and nine expeditions, and three concerts, including a solo performance from the headmaster.

Many new activities were started over a short period; a cricket pitch was created, followed by a rugger pitch and then a football pitch. If trees were in the way, the Headmaster would fell them and clear the ground with the help of the boys, and there was a repeated 'can do' attitude towards any task upon which the school turned its attention. A new boarding house was designed, built and filled with twenty boys, and then attention was turned to a new schoolhouse extension, which was duly built. A carpenter's shop was built, as well asa new covered playground and stables for boys who owned horses. The school offered tennis, fives and athletics in addition to swimming and rowing in the nearby canal. A cycling and running track was added around the cricket field.

The Daniels brothers enjoyed this rich tapestry of education in a fast-moving environment and thrived. One of the subjects debated by the Literary Society while Sidney was there was Proportional Representation, a subject that was to be so

131

much a part of Sidney's life in later years following his retirement from the Judicial Service and his move and interest in politics. In the 1930s Wycliffe appealed for prizes to award at Speech Days and Sidney sponsored an award for the best essay written by a boy on the topic of Proportional Representation. The award was presented for many years, which was Sidney's personal thank you. The Field Club organised many trips to various places of local interest to study and observe. One trip to the Roman Villa at Chedworth, by train to Cirencester, followed by a walk to Cheltenham and back to Stonehouse by train may have kindled other interests in the boys, for much later John Stewart was to be very involved in Woodchester Roman Pavement and Woodchester glass, and Harold had interests in flora and fauna. The Field Club also created a collection of over 2,000 items that they discovered, to form a school museum, and later John Stewart was to become involved in Stroud Museum from its inception. The boys were encouraged to organize the expeditions themselves and developed skills for self-sufficiency and organisation, budgeting and communication. The advent of photography as a mainstream hobby resulted in the building of a darkroom at the school, and later both John Stewart and Harold were keen photographers, the latter spending many hours at weekends travelling the county photographing plants, natural scenes and buildings. Many of his photos are now in the local Records Office.

Wycliffe was closely associated with the Methodist Church and some of the masters were Methodist preachers, active in meetings and rallies. The boys were involved and would assist in local services and became instrumental in the re-opening of Saul Chapel. Prayer meetings were a regular occurrence in school and there was a great emphasis placed on religious and moral values, together with service to others.

For the first eight years of Wycliffe there was a continual building programme, and so the boys will have been fascinated by the techniques and skills employed. They were always encouraged to get involved and Frederick was years later recognized by the school, when he joined the Governing Body, for his knowledge of building, together with his 'abilities to command a frugal approach'. But most importantly the school developed the boys into practical, well-grounded, well-educated and financially astute young men, ideally prepared for their careers in Joseph's engineering business. In addition, they were confident in mixing with boys of a social class to which the family now aspired and learned how to be young gentlemen. But probably the most important feature was their self-belief and a confidence that would take them and their business to great heights.

Sidney was exceptional in his abilities, but his less practical bias always ensured he was destined for great things. John Stewart passed his Junior Honours before leaving to join his father, Joseph, in the family business. He had the position of Probationer, or Under-Prefect at school, while his younger brother, Frederick, was a Prefect. Harold was a Probationer and both passed their Junior Honours.

Britain was prospering in the latter parts of the Victorian era: wealth was being created and a 'new rich' were coming of age. The key to the future lay in one's children, and education was crucial in determining their future paths. Much of the 'new money' was created in the cities, and primarily it was London that faired best. But London was not a good place to bring up children: sanitary conditions were poor, the air was full of smog often leading to thick fogs, streets were dirty and living conditions cramped. In addition, the 'new rich' tended to be busy people; true to their roots, they were workers and time was needed running their expanding businesses. Working hours were long, there was little social time, and family time was limited. Parents wanted their children to have a better education than they had had, and so it was a natural progression that children would be sent away to a boarding school in the country to achieve as good an education as possible.

G.W. chose Stonehouse as a place to create his school because of its rail links: it was an important interchange on the Midland line and the GWR line, and thus readily accessible to the big cities. It is interesting to note an advertising booklet from the time for a private girls' school, also in Stonehouse, highlights the sanitary conditions and the lofty, airy rooms as the most important issues, while the academic subjects are not of such great importance. Indeed, with death rates in childhood at such high rates, survival of children was paramount for the future of family businesses, and one's own care in old age, above simply learning.

However, the school academic results were good and the school prospered under the leadership of the Sibley family, always running a tight ship whilst embracing change and offering the very best of education. Connections with Old Wycliffians were maintained and their stories were published in *The Star*, Wycliffe's newspaper for past boys, including some from Sidney in India.

Life at the school ran in the family and W.A.Sibley became head in 1912. W.A's son T.M.Sibley was to join the school as a master and obtained his Scoutmaster's warrant in 1908 while living with the Cadburys in Birmingham. The earliest troops were formed at Wycliffe in 1909 with five patrols and thirty-six boys by 1910, which also saw the first camp on the banks of the River Wye. Expeditions were to become a regular feature of the boys' activities, both through the Scouts and other school trips by public transport or bicycle. WAS excelled in organisation and from initial confines of England he was soon taking large groups to explore Ireland or on cycling expeditions to the Alps.

From the inception of the school by G.W. in 1882 with Sidney starting in its first year, the bond between the school and the Daniels family became great, resulting in four generations of the family attending the school. There were a total of thirteen Daniels family members at the school in forty-four of the first seventy-six years of Wycliffe College's history. Sidney's results and ultimate rise to Judge in the Indian Civil Service was a significant achievement for the school and played a part in furthering the school's cause, but all the boys enjoyed their time and went on to achieve great things.

Frederick had enjoyed his time at Wycliffe and valued his education and so it was a natural choice that they would choose Wycliffe again for his sons, Eric and Lionel. Lionel excelled academically, doing well in the Sciences and Maths. He also enjoyed the activities and acquired a love of cycling and the outdoors. Both he and Eric were keen Scouts and took part in the Scouting trips.

Chapter 21. Boy Scouts

In 1907 the Baden Powell Scouting movement formed, based around a book that he wrote called Scouting for Boys, to impart useful skills that he had learned during the Crimean War. The Daniels family were always interested in youth and Clara Ada was involved with the school and the family were always keen to look after the welfare of the community. This was the start of a close relationship between the Daniels and Scouting for many years.

Rodborough Boy Scouts 1909

In 1909, Frederickk Lionel, now thirty-two, and known as Fred, together with Mr Frank Shaylor and Rev. C. E. Watson, set up a Scout troop at Rodborough Tabernacle. This would have been one of the first in Gloucestershire. Fred was officially registered as the Assistant Scout Master on 20 January 1910. The first public appearance in May 1910 was at the Church Pageant and they celebrated Peary and Cook, the first explorers to the North Pole, with a carnival procession from the Tabernacle to the Daniels field. In the early days there was little structure to the organisation. There were never any subs; funds would have been provided by the Daniels or through fundraising such as street collections, but the boys built their own hut for meetings on ground provided, and learned the camp-craft skills as laid down in the book. The annual Bonfire Night celebrations were held on the Daniels field with the bonfire built by the boys, collecting rubbish from the area. In addition, Scouts supported those in need, collecting prescriptions and tidying gardens.

On Easter Day 1916 a visit by Sir Robert and Lady Baden Powell inspected the parade outside the Tabernacle, and to mark the event a copse of oak, beech and fir

135

trees were planted near the 'lonely tree', close to the spot where George Whitefield had preached in the open on the Common.

The Rover Den was built in 1936 on land owned by the Tabernacle. Lionel became Rover Leader. In the early forties Baden Powell again visited and at Christmas 1946 more trees were planted by Lionel Daniels in a dedication ceremony at the spot where the copse had originally been planted. Unfortunately many of the trees died, as had the original trees, probably due to exposure on the top of the Common and so they were replaced with the hardier varieties that can be seen today.

Plaque at the place on Rodborough Common where the copse is located and the 'lonely tree' with the copse in the background.

A troop of Sea Scouts was started just prior to World War II, which was led by Eric Daniels. During the war the troops were discontinued as leaders were called up for military service; however, the older boys joined the Air Raid Precaution Messenger Service.

Lionel was awarded the Silver Acorn and Eric the Medal of Merit. Frederick was Honorary Treasurer of Gloucestershire when he died.

In the mid-thirties a 4cwt replica of an old Cotswold Milestone – the XXIXth milestone marking 1936 as the twenty-ninth year of the Scout Movement – was quarried from Minchinhampton Common and sent 13,000 miles to Australia.

The milestone was a gift from the Scouts of Stroud and Tetbury to the Scouts of Randwick, NSW, which owes its origin directly to the village of Randwick in the Stroud district and to one of the village's sons, Simeon Pearce, in particular.

Simeon Pearce, one of the early emigrants to Australia, is accepted as the founder of the NSW city in 1844. He was its first mayor and built the church of St Jude's there. Descendants of his family still live in the Stroud area.

136

Because there was no Scout troop in Randwick at the time, the Stroud district undertook the 1937 enterprise. It began one Saturday afternoon with a trek cart haul of the Minchinhampton stone by Rodborough Scouts from the old Crane Quarry.

The quarry has long since been filled in, and was from where the stone used to build Randwick Church had come. It was taken to the Art Memorial Company in Stroud who carved the inscription. It read 'XXIX milestone to the 1st Randwick, NSW, greetings from Stroud and Tetbury Boy Scouts, Gloucestershire, 13,000 miles'. (Crane Quarry was close beside the road on the Stroud side of Tom Long's Post).

After being put on display in the town, the milestone was loaded on to a rail truck at Stroud Great Western Railway Station for London. Loading took place under the direction of Netlam Bigg, who ran Handicapped Scouts at Standish Hospital, and Harry Haines, Rodborough Scoutmaster.

The stone was given free passage to Sydney by Peninsula and Oriental SS Co., and eventually erected in the grounds of St Jude's Church, Randwick.

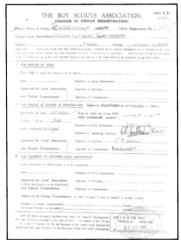

*Change of registration form
1948 with   Frederick Daniels
Scoutmaster
and Fred's Medal of Merit
record card dated 1947.*

Everyone involved in Scouting knew of the Daniels involvement and the organisation felt the loss of Fred and Eric when they died. In 1909 they had started Scouts and by 1937 they had a parade with over 500 Scouts to welcome the Acting Chief Scout to Stroud; the impact was huge.

Fred played an active part in the Scout movement for forty years, both in the troop he started and at District level; at his death in 1950 he was Honorary Treasurer for Gloucestershire District. The Scouting movement was extremely popular: in the early days they had so many Scouts that they had to stand in lines. Eric was extremely popular and was remembered for his camp-fire stories; he was also great fun and would often take the boys in his car. However, he was colour-blind and relied on the lads to tell him the traffic light colours – they were not always truthful!

Joseph Lionel also played a big part in Scouting and was awarded the Medal of Merit in 1942 and the Silver Acorn, the highest award possible, in 1957. Lionel started cubs in Stroud and, another generation on, my father, Peter was involved with Nailsworth Scouts and his brothers David Lionel and John Arnold were also Scouts. David started the Forest Green Scout troop in 1951 by which time he was Queen Scout having been in the Wycliffe troop for many years. The Daniels family were always interested in developing youngsters, be it funding local schools building science labs, the setting up of an exchange with a town in Germany or the apprenticeships in the factory.

Chapter 22 Red Letter Day

In 1949 Frederick Lionel, known as Fred, was taken ill. He was still a driving force in the business, Joint Managing Director and Chairman of Daniels (Cam) Ltd and a well-known and respected public figure. He had a keen interest in local government and at the time was Chairman of Stroud District Council.

He had been on the Stroud District Council since the boundary changes of 1936, and Chairman of the Highways and Town Planning Committee and a member of the Finance Committee. He was Chairman of The Stroud District Water Board and member of the Stroud District Planning Committee and the District Joint Sewerage Committee. For over thirty years he was a Governor of the Stroud Secondary Schools and member and Chairman of the Rodborough Group of Council Schools. He was a Rotarian and founder member of Stroud Rotary. He was a Justice of the Peace. He was a foundation Governor and member of the Executive Council of Wycliffe College. He was on the Management Board of Stroud General Hospital until it came under State control in 1948. He was also Chairman of the District Road Safety Committee, President of the Western Section of the Institute of Production Engineers, member of the Gyde Orphanage Management Committee, Stroud Juvenile Employment Committee and also served as a magistrate on the Stroud Bench. He was a Nonconformist and had a lifelong association with Rodborough Tabernacle, where he was a member of the deaconate, the choir, Church Treasurer and Sunday School Superintendent. He was also Chairman of the Executive Committee of the Gloucestershire and Herefordshire Congregational Union. In 1909 he formed one of the first Boy Scout troops. His knowledge of the countryside and interest in archaeology were profound and he was judge of the wild flowers section of Stroud Show, served on the Committee of Stroud Museum and was a Fellow of the Geological Society. Two of his main recreations were singing and bowling. For fifty years he was member of the Stroud Choral Society and he was Captain and President of Rodborough Bowling Club.

In 1942 he had celebrated his fifty years working at T.H. & J. Daniels, but because of the war the celebration was limited. To mark the event a photograph was taken with the staff with whom he worked. The photograph also shows the newest factory on the site; he was responsible for managing its build and oversaw all the planning.

Staff of Daniels photographed to mark Frederick's fifty years of service.

In 1950 Frederick Daniels, as Chair of the Stroud Urban District Council, was behind a visit to Stroud by Her Royal Highness Princess Elizabeth, before she became Queen. The family were proud of what had been achieved in Stroud by the people of Stroud and felt that a visit would be a tremendous boost and accolade. The family had been behind the visits years before of Baden Powell and knew of the effects that visits created. And this was in many respects for Fred a culmination of a life's work, creating a Stroud fit for a Royal visit. He organised the visit with precision and tried to ensure that she met as many people and groups as possible. In the event many thousands of people lined the route and factories were shut for the day. The event was a huge success, not just on the day but in terms of the standing within the political establishment and raising the national profile.

However, Fred was not well in the run-up to the visit. He had been taken ill in November 1949, and had briefly tried to return to work but had suffered a relapse. But he was determined that he would run the event, carry out his civic duties and escort Her Royal Highness on her visit. His doctor instructed him not to, saying that the visit would kill him, but he remained determined and the peril to his health was not made public. He disobeyed his Doctors orders.

Her Royal Highness Princess Elizabeth with Frederick Daniels, Councillors and Dignitaries

Princess Elizabeth with the Cadets. Fred on the right.

On 9 March he carried out his role, introducing the Council and other organisations, and taking lunch with her at the Imperial Hotel. In his address to Her Royal Highness he had said that the day was A Red Letter Day for Stroud and for him personally, and set the crown on a life's work; he announced his intention not to seek re-election at the May elections. He attended her on the walk around to meet the huge crowds that had gathered to see her and on to the train station for her train back to London. By now he was in great suffering and returned to the Imperial Hotel for a rest before returning home to go back to bed.

He died at 11.30 the next morning, 10 March 1950. The public were never told that he knew this would be his last engagement.

Chapter 23. The "DANARM" Chainsaw

In 1940 T.H. & J. Daniels patented a machine for felling trees and cutting them into logs. It comprised a chain saw, a gearbox, an internal combustion engine and an engineering solution to allow trees to be chopped up vertically.

The story of the chainsaw varies: in one version Lionel Daniels had travelled to London to meet with J. Clubley-Armstrong. He introduced him to a gentleman who had the idea for a chainsaw; in another, the plans were passed to him on a bridge in a secret rendezvous and it had German plans that were smuggled out of Germany.

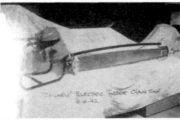 

The first 1942 electric chain saw and the 1944 version with petrol engine.

The saw, known as the DANARM, the name taken from DANIELS – ARMSTRONG, was to revolutionise the world of de-forestation. The first models in 1942 had an electric engine; then in 1944 a petrol version was produced using the Villiers 2-stroke engines, the first was a 250cc but different versions were produced from 80cc up to 350cc. The first version used a 39 inch cutting bar and was a 2 man lift. Models were introduced with longer cutting bars and the more powerful motors with the larger models capable of taking cutter bars up to seven feet in length to use on bigger trees.

Many of the early saws were supplied to War Office specification for use in jungle battle areas, but they later became widely used commercially. Examples exist today in museums as far away as Australia, which was a good market for the saw. The result was that the Daniels family travelled widely to support their local sales outlets.

The engine from a 1940's 2-man lift saw and the Whipper from 1950.

The DANARM Junior MK1 was introduced in 1945, incorporating the Villiers 98cc '8F' 2-stroke engine, the saw weighed about 28lb a one man lift!. A year later the newer version featured a diaphragm carburettor, which enabled the saw to be used easily by at any angle. The Tornado was introduced which was more powerful. This model became famous worldwide.

Around 1950 the Whipper was introduced powered by a JAP 80cc engine. It featured a wire pull/recoil starter and an automatic chain lubrication system. The Fury followed in 1953 with the 5F engine and a year later the 8F engine., however this was the first direct driven chainsaw without an additional chain.

In the 1960s and 1970s DANARM developed their own engines with a selection of 125cc, 110cc, 71cc and 55cc models, and later incorporated an anti-vibration system, using coil springs. Saws became much lighter in weight as magnesium castings were used extensively for the larger components.

During the later years of manufacture, which ceased in 1984, the company used its technology for other products and also bought in complimentary products from other suppliers and produced cultivators, brush cutters, hedge trimmers, lawnmowers, pumps and generators as well as chainsaws from TML, Pioneer and Komatsu Zenoah.

143

A press article on the Junior saw and a collection of saws.

In 1991 the then owner of DANARM, Linton Park plc, planned to terminate the company. However, the present Managing Director, who had been employed by T.H. & J. Daniels and DANARM since 1958, decided to continue the DANARM name. With Linton Park's agreement DANARM MACHINERY commenced trading in 1992. Most of the present ranges of products are imported from the Japanese manufacturing Company KAAZ Corporation with whom DANARM had a thirty-year association.

Patent:

Abstract of GB539956 539,956. Chain saw machines. DANIELS, Ltd., T. H. and J., and DANIELS, J. L. April 24, 1940, No. 7392. [Class 145 (ii)] A machine for felling trees and cutting them into logs comprises a chain saw 1 supported by a guide plate 8 which is detachably secured to the gear-box 4 of the driving unit, the gear-box being angularly adjustable about the driving shaft so that the saw may be used for horizontal, vertical, or inclined cutting whilst the driving unit which comprises an internal combustion engine 3 is maintained in a vertical position. The guide plate has both edges similarly curved and grooved so as to be reversible, and replaceable hardened steel bearing strips are provided in the base of the grooves. The guide plate is attached to the gearbox by a pin and keyhole slot arrangement together with a locking plate which is extended at 4b to form a work stop. The supporting bracket 6 at the outer end of the saw incorporates a tank 6a for lubricant which is fed on to the saw through a channel 6b in the guide plates. A stretcher bar 31 serving also as a saw guard and sufficiently thin to pass through the saw cut may be pivoted as shown.

Chapter 24 Jungle Toys of London

In 1903 the first 'teddy bear' as we know them was born from Steiff in Germany and started a new industry making bears. The bears became hugely popular in America, where 'Teddy' Roosevelt had been unable to shoot a bear on a hunting trip and hence the teddy name had been born.

Edith Mabel Daniels, daughter of Joseph and Clara Ada Isacke, went to Stratford Abbey School where her artistic skills developed. She went on to the West Kensington School of Art in London and it was here whilst studying that she went to London Zoo to draw the animals with a friend Grace Playell. During the visit a 'black cat' crossed their path, which they sketched with caption 'pussy, keep your tail up'. Later they decided to mould it in clay, before using the mould to produce a template design and a soft toy. The First World War had just begun and they presented it to a General heading a recruitment drive and it appeared life size on the front of his car. Shortly afterwards they received an order for 6 more of the 'mascots' from the Army and the business was born.

Before the war teddy bears had been imported from Germany, but this ceased creating a need for companies within the UK to fill the gap. We are not entirely sure exactly when it started, one report says Edith worked for other manufacturers first before starting, and the earliest advert in catalogues dates to 1916, but by 1919 it was run on a co-operative basis with over 13 assistants. They started with cats, including the 'black cat', kittens and patriotic lions but it soon developed into wide menagerie of animals. They were all formed in clay before a pattern being produced and Edith was absolutely fastidious about accuracy, she was once asked why they didn't make teddy bears and replied that they were not realistic. One family member recalls how one bale of fur had stripes that were 'too wide' to be used on the tiger, and so it was returned to the manufacturer.

British toys appealed to an American market and many were sent to the US, but they were also exported to India, Australia, Canada and South Africa. At this time there were few toyshops in England and Edith was fortunate to secure Harrods as an outlet, along with supplying direct to order and through large department stores.

The company started in Richmond Road, Earls Court, but outgrew the premises and moved to Brompton Road which was the ideal base to supply the growing demand in the UK and America. The inspiration for the designs came from the London Zoo: Edith insisted that the animals had to be lifelike and went to great lengths to obtain fur fabric that was realistic in colour, patterning and fur length. Edith always carried out one activity and that was the task of affixing the glass eyes. The positioning of the eyes gave the toys their character and she liked to see the characters come to life.

All the animals were hand-made and as the business grew outworkers were used as there was never more than 20 staff. This was essential as the demand was at its peak at Christmas and it would not have made sense to have a permanent force through the year.

Mary by Gwynedd Ray, Rabbits in Red Cross uniforms for the Second World War..

In 1921 A.A. Milne's wife Daphne bought a bear from Harrods for their son Christopher Robin. Over the next couple of years Piglet, Eeyore, Kanga & Roo were added and inspired A.A. Milne to write *Winnie the Pooh*, which was published in 1926. The book became a huge success. Tigger, who appears in a later book, was a Jungle Toy tiger, probably bought from Harrods. Later, when his son had grown up, the original toys were given by A.A. Milne to his American publisher and are now currently a major attraction on display at the Library in New York, including the Jungle Toy tiger.

In the 1930's it is said that Edith and Grace were very proud when two lions were presented to the Princess Elizabeth and her sister Princess Margaret. Another famous owner was Winston Churchill where his soft toy panda can still be found today in his study at Chartwell. The story goes that he used it to mark the location when he removed a book so that he would know where to put the book back.

Bingo Bears came in several sizes and the smallest could easily fit in a pocket. There is a report of Bingo being given to a pilot who took part in the Battle of Britain, and another who accompanied his owner in a Mosquito on over 50 operations over Germany and together they won the DFC (Distinguished Flying Cross). The story of the teddy went viral on the Internet.

Roald Dahl's first daughter had a collection of Jungle Toy rabbits. She sadly died of measles aged 7 which affected him deeply.

Tigger and friends in the New York Library and another from the author's collection.

Jungle Toys labels. To the characteristic label was added the registration number before being replaced in later years by the stitched label, usually on the foot and the tag stitched into a seam.

A Jungle Toy Tiger, Lion and Dog; A Polar Bear. Author's collection.

In 1929 they exhibited at the British industries Fair; advertising as manufacturers of Soft Toy Animals, best quality only. Dog Models, with the characteristics of each breed, are a speciality. A 1927 advert shows 'Sing-Sing' a Pekinese dog and 'Dash' a Black Cocker Spaniel, other reports name Alsatians, Chow-Chows, Samoyeds' Irish, Airedales, Cairns, Fox Terriers, Sealyhams, Sheepdogs, Corgis and Greyhounds.

In 1928 Bingo Bear was introduced, which was to become their bestseller. The range contained a number of bears, including Bingham Bear, made of mohair. They also came in a range of sizes. These were popular despite being a Koala and not a bear. At its peak the business had about twelve people making toys for shipment all over the world. Harrods was supplied with some unique designs.

"Jungle" toys that were admired and bought by the royal visitors.

A newspaper clipping about the Jungle Toys for the Princesses Elizabeth and Margaret and an advert for the 'Quinns' purchased by Her Majesty the Queen and the Duke of Kent.

There was a wide range of original designs of wild and domestic animals and as well as toys they made, pyjama cases. They included lions, tigers, pandas, donkeys, monkeys, dogs, cats bears and rabbits. Some 'Beatrix Potter' style rabbits were advertised in catalogues as Benjamin and Belinda, he in a red felt jacket, she in an embroidered felt skirt that was specially made by a lady employed by the company to carry out embroidery. During World War II some of the rabbits made were dressed as Red Cross nurses. Also of particular interest there was 'Simba' a lion, 'Lena' the lioness and 'Cubby' a lion cub.

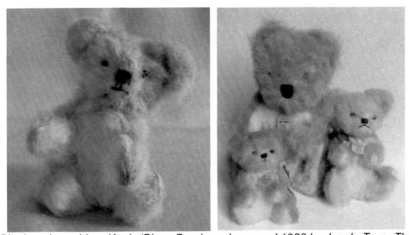

Bingham is an 11cm Koala 'Bingo Bear', made around 1930 by Jungle Toys. The 'Bingo Bears' in a range of sizes from the author's collection.

149

As well as business partner, Edith had a great personal companion in Grace Playle who worked alongside her in the business and designed many of the toys; she was a flamboyant individual who was always full of fun and in many ways a great foil for Edith, who was the businesswoman, domineering and rather formidable. Relatives remember Grace's vibrant dress sense that was in many ways as outlandish as the outfits they created for some of the animals.

Christmas was a very busy time. In those days shops opened on Christmas morning and parents would take children to the large stores to collect the Jungle Toys that had been made to order, so the activity to manufacture them was frenetic up until the last moments, as every toy had to be delivered to expectant children. Many of the toys were shipped to the US with the final shipment of toys not dispatched until Christmas Eve. But work continued on shipments for the London department stores through into Christmas Day morning. No child could be left out.

Afterwards, Edith and Grace always headed to Gloucestershire for Christmas with the Daniels family, often arriving just as the meal was being served, having fulfilled all the commitments, but completely exhausted.

A tall fox produced in a 'doll' format and the 'London Owl' characters. The Cricketer is dressed in Wycliffe School colours (minus gold!) and the Judge may be a reference to Sidney Daniels. Author's collection.

150

The business continued to prosper. A range of larger, doll-like toys were developed, including foxes and badgers; then at some stage a relationship with the London Owl Company resulted in a range of owls, based on the larger, one-foot doll format. Interestingly, there was a Judge, which may have been a reference to Sidney Daniels, an owl cricketer in early Wycliffe colours, a lady doctor, which was unusual and may have been a reference to Dr Helen Daniels, and a businessman, a reference to other Daniels members. They were dressed in quintessentially British costumes primarily for the American market, sold under the Jungle toys of London brand and boxed, indicating that they were for collectors as much as a toy. They became very popular in America.

Jungle toys were made until the 1970s by Edith who worked into her nineties. The business was still successful and she did not want to close it and eventually she found someone to take over the company. Edith died the week after they took over.

Edith Daniels in 1904 taken by John Stuart and a later photograph of unknown date. An advert for 'Jungle Toys' rabbits.

151

Chapter 25. The Dawn of a New Era

During the First World War, the entire production capacity had been turned over to military manufacture, resulting, as we have seen, with difficulties after the war finished. At the conclusion of the Second World War the directors were more aware of the potential problems that lay ahead. The business had survived the war and now had a strong cash flow and technical portfolio with which to move forward. The funds from Government contracts continued to flow into the business for some time after the war; this helped, but what they needed was more customers with new work.

After the previous war, and again after the great depression they had worked on two fronts, the first was to actively seek work from any contacts they could, making calls to everyone they knew, and the second was to look overseas for companies requiring agents or wanting to manufacture in Britain. This they repeated with great success, but additionally this time the Government contracts continued to flow – not for product but for technical know-how.

The company's standing within government departments was high, they recognized the technical abilities of the company and as a result they continued to place military contracts. During the war, Germany had stepped up its technical development activities and for five years there had been little communication within the global scientific community to enable others to follow progress. The British Army was therefore tasked with obtaining the technical 'secrets' for the advantage of companies in the UK and enlisted support from Daniels.

To help make this possible, Lionel was made a Colonel in the British Army and travelled widely to companies in Germany with the army throughout 1946 and '47. However, rather than drawings, much of the documentation was coded in numerical formats to ensure that, had it fallen into British hands, it would have been useless. Fortunately, Jan Stiassny, being an extremely clever mathematician, was able to decipher the codes, and from these drawings or technical papers were produced. Some of the equipment was military hardware: rockets and launchers, armoury and ammunitions. In some cases models of the German equipment were made in the factory for the use of the army, and equipment was being made and shipped to Woolwich Arsenal in London where it was tested by the army well into the 1950s. The activities were extremely sensitive and the work was carried out on site in secret.

One development was for a 'spinner' that measured the amount of 'spin' a bullet had leaving a gun. It was discovered that if a bullet spun it would travel straighter and shooting was more accurate. As a result, new guns were developed for the British Army with new rules indicating 'shoot to maim' rather than 'shoot to kill'. Many of the guns developed are still standard military issue. But there is a story which relates that a shipment of product that was sent out from the factory; apparently it went missing on its way to Woolwich and was never found.

An Admiralty 'Spinner'.

In addition to the work in Germany, Lionel visited both Egypt and Israel in 1948, requiring him to have two passports, a situation that was unheard-of in those days. He visited Palestine on plastic moulding projects and recounted how his work was in hot conditions in the middle of a desert near an oasis.

His children saw little of him at this time, and indeed they are unable to say much about his work, but they recall some of his stories and were introduced to philately through the stamps he collected from the countries he visited.

The work carried out by the Daniels was extremely important to the country and continued for some time. Peter Daniels recalls that, in the 1960s, newly into his role in the company, he was asked to show a foreign visitor around the site. He did so and gave him an extensive tour for several hours, following which the visitor was arrested. Peter, shocked by the developments, was questioned by the police for some time about the visitor and it transpired that he was a Russian spy sent to gather military secrets. Nothing was said afterwards about the event and the fate of the spy was unknown.

Shortly after the war in 1951 Stroud twinned with Duderstadt in Germany. It is likely that Lionel will have been visiting the town as part of his work. What is interesting is that a company Ottobock in Duderstadt was manufacturing prosthetics for war victims, but that there was a shortage of wood. In 1953 the company pioneered the manufacture of them using plastics. The likelihood is they used Daniels presses, Lionel would have understood the huge importance to the rebuilding of Germany. The company remains the a world leader to this day.

153

However, the policy Daniels put into place of taking on agency agreements for companies in foreign countries, providing and sometimes manufacturing their product in Britain, and the policy of setting up overseas agencies, offices and working with companies abroad to grow their international sales, proved highly successful. There were a great many agreements put in place that yielded benefit over the coming years. Daniels was emerging an international company with an enviable reputation.

The result was that the factory was not only kept busy, but was soon not big enough. In addition to the work for the military, there was the supply of piece-parts and bespoke designs for industry; the manufacture of chain saws and the plastics and rubber industries were growing with demands for ever-increasingly complex equipment. Family members recall the chainsaws in manufacture with many hundreds of saws at various stages of assembly in rows and rows filling factory units. Lionel regularly brought home new variants of the saw that had been built as models in the design lab for testing. In the grounds of the family home was a small wood and the boys would try out each new model by felling a tree, which they would then use to chop up for firewood to heat the family home until the next version of saw in a few weeks. If they managed to break the saw then it was back to the drawing board for the design team.

The demand for presses and injection moulding equipment continued to increase; during the war many manufacturers of consumer products had turned to plastics to replace metal, which had been limited in supply. Now, as the business started to return to normal, the trend to plastics continued as the advantages in cost-cutting were being recognized. The initial tooling costs for each product manufactured were high, but the costs per item made were then much lower than traditional manufacturing methods. Alfred Herbert Ltd, with their large industrial customer base, were also finding increasing demand for plastics from motor manufacturing, clothing, home products – in fact, from every industry.

Prototype injection machine in the old factory. Daniels designed the Herbert 2360 type 'S' prototype.

Alfred, who by now was in his seventies, could see the growing importance of plastics and respected the technical abilities of the Daniels, working closely with them on development. His investment was focused primarily on the applications and the production of the bespoke tools, although he marketed and sold some of

154

his 'own machines'. He had one plant working entirely on tool production, development and testing.

At the Daniels site, in addition to their own presses, they manufactured the Alfred Herbert equipment, which was then shipped to Coventry for testing and configuration for the customer's application. But the machines were large and so manufacturing space on the Daniels site was at a premium.

The business was well organised and was successful, but there were two problems facing growth. The first was that, as the Government had identified during the war, the factory was at its capacity, and secondly, some of the businesses that bought some of the more traditional products from T.H. & J., were experiencing funding issues of their own.

From the perspective of managing the business, the end of the war was a turning point for the running of the company. Lionel now took charge with Frederick and John becoming less involved, turning their attention to their other activities within the community and their hobbies. But they continued to take an active interest in the company and helped to form the strategy that could deliver growth in the various markets.

An annual meeting known as 'Cowley Manor' (the name of the venue where it was held near Cheltenham), was instigated and involved many of the key members of the workforce as well as the management. This helped to set the plan for the longer term and helped to encourage the workforce to meet goals to which they had been a party, known today as team-building.

Staff photograph at Cowley Manor.

The continued success of business resulted in a good cash-flow. Extending the factory and building new facilities was not possible for some time after the war as the materials, which themselves were scarce, were diverted to building housing. So another strategy started to develop, to acquire businesses that used the more traditional products from the foundry and metalworking workshops and businesses where there was synergy of manufacture in the same areas. This would keep the traditional parts of Daniels busy whilst enabling the management to focus on the engineering, sales and development on the plastics and more modern parts of the industry.

Eventually building restrictions eased and new factory workshops were built to cope with the manufacturing space confines, and any manufacturing businesses bought could be utilised for other assembly work if needed, instead of the high reliance placed on sub-contractors that had been the case. The new buildings included an extension to Thomas Falconers building, a number of infill sheds and more buildings further up the slope.

Fern Cottage, Joseph's original house, had been used as offices for the Drawing Office and Administration for many years, but it was too small. Harold's 'Whitecroft' near Nailsworth had also been turned into office space and was now used for Pratt Daniel, but that was full. In a post-war Britain short of builders and building materials the Government prioritized building for industrial purposes through a licencing system; so when a new office block and drawing office was authorized in

156

the late 1940s, a bold step was taken to create a solid brick and block building that was uniquely different from the more usual buildings constructed on site. It was a big step for the company in that it represented a very modern face for the business. Until then, buildings on site were basically cost-efficient sheds, but this was a grand, brick-built office suite designed in the latest style. It was a statement that Daniels felt they had arrived. At its inception, Frederick and John Stuart were at the pinnacles of their careers; they enjoyed the pomp and ceremony of Council and Masonry, and needed to create a building that formed an epitaph to their work. In addition, the hard work through the war activities had created the profits they required to create the visionary building and there was a confidence throughout the country that was palpable. However, that is not to say it was impractical; it was desperately needed to house the management activities which were growing as Government were producing increasing rafts of regulation: the Drawing Office, which was under strain for new products and product variants, the Purchasing Office and other Administration. Two identical upstairs offices looked out over the existing site, one for Frederick, the other for John.

The new office block with the sales demonstration room addition; the original entrance.

Unfortunately, by the time it was finished the building was too small and it was not long before an extension was built to create a purpose-built show room; this created an area where products could be shown off in a permanent demonstration area, something of which Frederick and John could be proud.

By the early 1950s, both Frederick and John had passed away. The company was now under the leadership of Lionel. The offices were still insufficient and so the salesroom was removed and a new wing built to house more office space. Lionel had found that the demonstration area was of little value because most of his customers were spread around the globe and few visited the site at Stroud. He was far more outwardly focused than the previous generation and now had a drive for growth.

In many ways the extension was also Lionel's way of putting his mark on the business. For many years he had been playing a key part in the business, but had been treated as junior: photographs taken at the time show him on the side-lines, whilst Frederick surrounded himself with his management, who in turn answered to Frederick and John.

Now he had to exert his authority on the business and show that the company had a future.

A wing was added with a new, grander entrance. Above were new offices for himself and his future sons. They faced a different direction, part facing the gates and the customers, part facing the old factory, but primarily looking out at the site where the next big factory unit was planned.

The extension was joined to the main building, but it was also slightly distanced from the old part; he distanced himself from the old management, without directly replacing them, but from his vantage point he could see the workers arrive and leave and see his managers' activities.

The new entrance as it was built and as it is today.

When his new offices were complete, Lionel organised an opening ceremony and his mother, Winifred, officially opened the new wing. This put the seal of approval on the project by the previous generation of which she was by now the last. What is telling is that the photographs taken of the day were of Lionel with the workers and not management.

*The new office block being officially opened by Winifred with Lionel as M.D.
overseeing and Lionel with the administrative staff.*

The 'new' administration block with the factory to the right. A car park was now necessary (left) with the bike sheds.

The change of leadership at the top of the company must have been difficult for the existing managers. They had grown up within the company under the previous generation and were used to a relaxed, communicative company with many Daniels family members to consult. Now Lionel was an autocratic leader, who had no other Daniels members to consult and was keen for change to take the business forward. He was already busy with his existing responsibilities but now had more, his time was at a premium and so had little time for managers and meetings. He was not into pomp and ceremony, and structure for the sake of it, but hard work. He disliked Freemasonry because it took away his managers during a working day for no what he perceived as no gain to the business. He treated all his staff equally and did not put his managers on a pedestal in the way that they had been treated by the previous generation, choosing rather to make them earn respect from the workforce.

In fairness, the management on the shop floor liked his style; he was personally involved in the day-to-day running of the business and his decisiveness helped smooth their activities, and it was successful as the business continued to grow.

He was keen on new development as the lifeblood of an engineering company and was an active member of many engineering organisations. His travel brought

160

to the fore new ideas, which he introduced to his engineering development team. The company had amassed some excellent technical experts who could turn their hand to all manner of new concepts. During this time many new inventions were made and the patents filed by Daniels were numerous, mostly to do with injection moulding and presses for the plastics industry.

He was keen on collaboration with other businesses, both in development and in manufacture, work being passed between the Daniels plant and other companies within the valley to overcome workload peaks, and to achieve best manufacturing practice.

In the main factory he knew every employee by name, and when he was on site, he was regularly to be found on the shop floor or in engineering finding out how to maintain a fast throughput of work; he worked with the technical staff to resolve problems, sorting out funds for equipment or manpower when necessary. People recall how busy and fast- moving the factory was; the foundry working to capacity was noisy and hot. The purchasing department was next to his office; materials were essential to the business, and it was where the money went, along with labour, which he also tracked. But he was also the main salesman; he would be out visiting companies and brokering deals, working alongside the sales team to ensure they won as much business as possible.

The business was becoming increasingly global, with Lionel travelling further across the world to discuss sales projects. His secretary is remembered as the height of efficiency, some of his trips involving some complicated travel arrangements to remote locations when global travel was unusual. In the Daniels household Lionel would appear at the breakfast table to announce he was back, but the gathered group had been unaware that he had been to America the day before for the day. Trips to Australia and the Far East were not unusual and one trip of 42 days took him to New York, Denver, San Fransisco, Honolulu, Fiji, Aukland, Sydney, Bankok, Beirut, Rome and Frankfurt. He continued to visit companies, seeking business at a relentless pace, in exactly the way he had when he first started with the company, but on a global scale.

Australia was a particularly important country, having imposed duties on imported goods, he set up manufacturing facilities for Daniels products within the country.

The family were always keen to embrace technology and the use of a helicopter was no exception, although it was too expensive for regular journeys. The company continued to grow through the 1950s and grew in workforce to a peak of over 1300 workers on site, with the building of the new workshops and offices.

The offices built in the late 1940s on the left, extended in the 1950s to the right. Note the metal casement windows. Lionel's office upstairs middle window: looking out over the entrance and up the site towards the future.

At this time, the Board of Daniels acted more to officialise Lionel's activities than to spearhead the business. Department heads carried out the paperwork that was required, an increasing workload as new legislation was introduced. The accounting requirements and staff welfare were a very different affair from the early days of the business, whilst Lionel ran the site with great enthusiasm and energy and with a hands-on style.

1960s advert for moulding equipment featuring a press; a Meterjet press in the factory, a 130 ton press; Daniels hydaulic press for injection moulding advertised for sale on the internet in 2011.

162

Under Lionel, T.H. & J. Daniels was a good employer: it recognised the importance of its people in the skills and enthusiasm they had. Aspirations were encouraged and the company supported staff wanting to learn more and better themselves; most of the technical staff had risen through the ranks and staff turnover was low. It was a good company to work for: the company was fair to employees and operated a Social Club, providing facilities such as a recreation area on the field above the factory. There were perks, such as a Christmas turkey, Christmas parties and employee loans. A profit-related bonus scheme was operated and a pension scheme in place to support those in retirement.

Members of Daniels '25' Club in 1956
workers having served the company for over 25 years.

Many employees remember their time at the company with fondness, and the Daniels family were generally popular and well respected pillars of society. As we have seen, the Daniels were Christians who believed in supporting local people and helping them control their own destinies, but they also supported the vulnerable members of society and employed many staff with disabilities. We know of six staff with major disabilities, including several who were blind, who worked on lathes, and an amputee, who was employed as a welder.

163

Herbert Harwood, Arthur Dalman & Jocelyn Brewer working blind on lathes and an unknown ex-soldier amputee welder.

T. H. & J. DANIELS, LTD., STROUD
HANDBOOK
Second Issue, 1951

1951 cover of the Staff Handbook

After church on a Sunday, Lionel would visit staff who were at home from sickness or other members of the community who were in need and if help was needed he would find a way of providing support: a Scout to do the shopping, a visit from the company nurse, or support in other matters. On occasion his sons joined him on his rounds. The Sunday lunch at the Daniels' house was a big affair and there were often over twenty partaking. Invitations would be passed out during the week to a wide variety of people, from visiting clergy to business men and staff members at every level – in reality, no-one knew how many were going to turn up and it made for a lively social mix of conversation.

The company supported the Stroud Hospital through charitable giving, but it also had its own health provision with a nurse onsite and a visiting doctor. Helen herself was a doctor, and although there is no evidence in her involvement at the factory, she continued to practise as a doctor from their home near the factory. Later, she became a popular speaker at women's meetings such as the WI, where she gave talks specifically aimed at supporting women with her medical knowledge in a time when many women's issues were 'taboo', and providing guidance on bringing up a family.

Lionel and Helen were seen as 'pillars of the society' and would be invited to open numerous church events, fairs and garden parties, whilst also being asked to get involved or to spearhead all sorts of activities. In effect, before the advent of TV, the family had celebrity status and would be treated with great respect and affection, opening fêtes and attending public events around Stroud.

However, Lionel felt the strain of running the company single-handed. His vision was always that his sons would join him in the business as soon as possible. There was never any discussion over whether they would go to university or study anything other than a route into engineering, having served apprenticeships. It is interesting that Lionel felt this way about university considering that he had been to university himself; it may have been his eagerness for them to start within the company, or it may have been that in his career he had been made to feel an outsider when he had started: all the other managers had risen through the apprenticeship route, putting him at a disadvantage technically in his earlier days. John and David duly left school and both served engineering apprenticeships, John at Alfred Herbert in Coventry, where there was a purpose-built school for the apprentices, and David at Fielding & Platt. It was Lionel's intention that all the boys would join the company, and that a strategy of acquisition would support this because each son could then have a business to run before eventually taking the reins at the mother company.

The business grew and continued to prosper and Lionel acquired businesses: by 1955 T.H. & J. Daniels had bought British Boiler Accessories (Daniels BBA), had a share in Leslie Hill (Stonehouse), had acquired the controlling interest in Pratt Daniel (Stanmore) Ltd and had bought Hill and Enderby in Cornwall.

In 1956 the company announced that for the first time the turnover for the company had exceeded £1M, and was making good profits. The asset value of the business was now £600,000.

165

Further company acquisitions followed, including Gordons on the outskirts of London and Sharples Centrifuges, both companies that T.H. & J. had worked with and made their products for many years.

But still the growth was constrained by a lack of manufacturing space. Plans were now drawn-up for a much larger workshop at the top of the site, next to the car-park. The design was again revolutionary affording lots of light inside a lofty space and designed to be multi-purpose. The project was to be financed by additional borrowing and the building was started. The project was completed reading for manufacturing in the early 1960's.

The new building.

Unyet whilst the growth and smooth running of the company can be attributed to Lionel for this period, the managers, staff and workers all worked together as one team. Lionel was often away for some time much of it travelling abroad, but he also travelled within the UK and regularly went up to London for meetings. He started to use a helicopter that was hired to speed up his travel.

Lionel was also busy in so many other ways: he was an active member of the Cotswold Players, an organisation spawned from a pageant held in Stroud Park in 1911 with the aim of bringing plays to the villages. From 1946 he was keen to see the Players acquire their own theatre as a base from which to operate, and he led the fundraising activities that, with generous support from the many friends of the players, resulted in a theatre. In 1951 they bought the Primitive Methodist Chapel in Parliament Street for £1,500, and, with plans drawn up by Edgar Leah, converted it to create a theatre, which has gone on to greater success and further expansion and modernisation, fulfilling its original intent. Today's website (cotswoldplayers.co.uk), says of Lionel:

"The success of the appeal was almost entirely due to the energy and devotion of the late Lionel Daniels and the many friends of the players who contributed handsomely to this fund and made it possible to put the work of conversion in hand."

Indeed, the description of a man with boundless energy is one that has been repeated often to me by many in relation to Lionel. He became involved in so many activities locally: he was heavily involved with Wycliffe College, particularly whilst his sons were at the school, and was on the Governing Body, Chairman at one stage, and took an active interest in the development of the buildings. He was also supportive when the school was given some machining equipment and set up a club for the boys to learn to use it. To support this, the Works Manager, Dyer, himself an old Wycliffian, was dispatched to teach the boys. Projects grew from small items that could be made in the workshop to take home to the building of a new boathouse and landing stage for the rowing club, a project supported by Lionel with the Works to call upon for any activities required.

But he also was involved in many other projects, such as the preservation of the Talyllyn railway in North Wales. The society was set up in 1951 to preserve the line and Lionel would drive up with his wife and boys at the weekend to help out. Lionel was a valuable member of the team because of his mechanical knowledge and his connections to get parts required for its reconstruction. Peter, his son, also describes how Lionel was a keen walker with his family and on one visit they were in the area when they came across a slate quarry. They entered the site to find it abandoned, but left exactly as it had been when the workers left.

Lionel was a keen gardener and with eleven acres to maintain at their house, Overden, it was a significant challenge. He would come home after a long day at work and after a quick tea, he would head out into the garden for the evening, often finishing after dark, using a torch to see until his work was complete. There was a gardener, but in reality it was too big a task for one. This was a time when Lionel could relax and unwind without the pressures of everyone wanting him, time to think and to plan. Occasionally during the holiday periods he would enlist the help from his sons, setting tasks that involved them digging a line each in a piece of ground, following on from the one in front; the slowest would be identified as falling behind, a technique probably aligned from the time-and-motion studies that were so popular at the time. At other times he would tender for the fence to be painted or for some other project to be done: the boys would bid for the work with the cheapest receiving the contract. I shudder to imagine what the quality of the final work may have been like, as the boys were so young, but it was all in jest and no mental damage was incurred.

In addition, Lionel was a Freeman of the City of London, and was a member of the exclusive St. James's Club opposite the Houses of Parliament; so he met many Members of Parliament and top people in the City of London, playing a part and helping to influence Government policy on industrial matters.

The Daniels also had many other interests, including an active interest in Stroud's Twinning Association with Duderstadt, Germany, and supported the youth exchange with Stroud, standing on the Stroud Youth Services Committee. This helped relations whilst giving local people an opportunity of wider experience. Daniels were always keen on supporting youth, and Lionel was involved in Stroud Technical College, Wycliffe College and various other organisations involved in apprenticeships and technical training.

He would always encourage youngsters, including his own family. At a very young age Peter went to Scotland to visit someone whom Lionel had met whilst walking in the glens, and stayed with him in his cottage. Peter and Philip cycled across France and crossed the Alps to Italy on a tandem soon after the war.

Lionel in a helicopter on the recreation field next to the site.

Chapter 26. Sudden Death

On 8 January 1958, Joseph Lionel Daniels. aged just fifty, was killed in a car crash on the A38 on the Derby bypass; his passenger was a business man, Pip Nelson, who survived but was seriously hurt, whilst driving home from a business meeting.

The Stroud News and Journal reported:

"(He) has long been honoured in the Stroud district, and much further afield, for the enterprise and drive displayed in industrial matters and for the energy and devotion given to religious and social causes.

Mr J. Lionel Daniels, whose tragic death is so universally mourned, was no exception to this. He followed in every way the admirable example set by his late father Mr F.L. Daniels, whose younger son he was, but he also revealed special qualities of his own..."

Lionel was Managing Director and was the key figure in the business, having run it for many years; he was involved in every aspect of the business and was the decision-maker. He had grown the business, which now owned other companies: Gordons, on the outskirts of London, Sharples Centrifuges and Pratt Daniels, as well as Hill & Enderby in Penzance.

At the inquest it was found that there was no fault on the part of Lionel: the accident was caused by the other driver, who survived the crash.

On the day of Lionel's funeral the Daniels factory was closed. A memorial service was held at Rodborough Tabernacle. The *Stroud News & Journal* lists the names of 800 people who attended and signed the condolence book, but there were many more, maybe thousands of people who joined the crowds to pay tribute. He was a leading pillar of society in his prime, an industrialist with global connections, involved in the Boy Scouts, having been awarded the Silver Acorn, on the boards of schools, Chair of Stroud & District Council, member of the Rotary Club, instrumental in the twinning organisation, President of the Cotswold Players and took part in Rodborough Tabernacle Players, a member of the West Region Advisory Council for broadcasting, a lay preacher taking a lifelong interest in the church and taking the mantle of several senior posts.

There were many tributes. The Cotswold Players said of him:

'The news of the so sudden death of our President has come as a tremendous shock and grief to the Players. It is no exaggeration to say that without his energy and generosity this building could never have become a theatre. The same qualities have made themselves manifest in all the many activities to which he devoted his life. We ourselves regard the Playhouse as his living monument, and although today we observe the tradition of the theatre we go on with a sense of mourning and loss for a man who, above all things, carried his strong faith from his early life.'

The *South Hanover Press*, a German newspaper said:

"(Lionel) was highly regarded here not only in youth circles but as one of the best known and best liked Englishmen. His passing tears a deep gap in international connections for both countries.'

Stroud News & Journal:

'Several local youth clubs have asked... if they can join in some form of permanent memorial to Mr Daniels and have made it obvious that his passing is a very great loss to them.'

Also printed in the paper alongside the tributes:

WISH

Because it is felt it should be his wish, the annual party for children of employees of Messrs. T.H. & J. Daniels was carried through on Saturday. In the past Mr Daniels has always played the part of Father Christmas.

Chapter 27. The Wilderness Years

By 1958 the business was doing well: turnover for T.H. & J. Daniels had reached over £1m with a net profit of around £100,000. Daniels (CAM) was producing £6,000 profits on £100,000 turnover, and the new business, Pratt Daniels, was producing a 20% return on the shares. In addition, the company owned a number of other companies, who in turn served a variety of markets and had in place a deal with Alfred Herbet PLC, where they acted as selling agents for Daniels presses, and brought assembly work of their own products to the Daniels factory. There was also a big investment in new assembly workshops with modern facilities on the site.

Inside the 'new' factory with assembly of Daniels Presses on the left and Herbert Injection Moulding Machines on the right.

Aerial View of the Factory.

'Meterjet' presses moulding rubber at Dunlop, Skelmersdale; 'Microjet' presses encapsulating electronic components at Ferranti, Barrow-in-Furness.

Paper core covering machines at Pirelli, Southampton; Plastics injection moulding machines made for Alfred Herbert and installed at Kodak, Stevenage.

Plastics presses moulding electrical parts at Ether, Biggleswade. Cylinder head assembly machine at Vauxhall, Luton.

Daniels 'Topformer' for production of thin-walled disposable containers, such as plastic cups and boxes.

We have seen that the connection with Alfred Herbert went back to the 1920/30s. His company was the largest machine tool supplier in the world, and he had many offices and factories in many countries as well as distributors. Alfred was also an

173

autocratic leader. He had no family to take over his business and so it was run by a board with his continued involvement, although in his later years he spent less time on it and more on other projects within Coventry, such as the Alfred Herbert Museum, his legacy to the city. But because of the nature of the work in Stroud there was a continued personal connection with him.

The 1960s & 70s were a time of great upheaval for engineering. Government legislation removed import tariffs; this resulted in increased competition from overseas, and they reduced the length of the working week, thus putting up labour costs. As a result, inflation took hold; this was difficult for businesses and difficult for household budgets. Workers now formed into unions, demanding more income and better working conditions, putting new pressures on businesses and diverting management time. The upper classes were associated with business and so attacks on companies were seen as attacks on the rich, which was acceptable. A raft of legislation was introduced by governments that now consisted of a new breed of people, many from backgrounds where business was despised. The governments of the time lost control of the economy and managed to create havoc with the industrial base of the country.

Traditionally, investment in business and industry had mostly come from the wealthy. However, the new age of politics was aimed at stripping the wealth from individuals. Death taxes paid by the Daniels, who were not wealthy by the standards of traditional land owners, were up to 80%. Business investment requirements increased as products became more complex, and industry fell behind foreign competition.

Alfred Herbert died in 1957. Over the next twenty years his business felt the full impact of the industrial change. Industrial growth was slowing; the car industry, the mainstay of Coventry industry, was subject to immense industrial strife. Closures, mergers and takeovers led to the eventual collapse of the industry into the 1970s. The Coventry economy was based on engineering and most were affected. Businesses could not respond quickly enough to the changes and product quality was affected. Design and development was starved of funding; bank funding was focused on short-term returns and capital was used in re-organisation to immediate profit gains. Most engineering industries suffered, and the decline hit Herberts because they were suppliers to engineering companies throughout the UK. In 1972 they made a loss of £2.5M, followed by further losses in 1973 and 1974. The business collapsed shortly afterwards, leaving many thousands of employees out of work.

By the late 1950s and early 1960s the Board at Herberts could see the problems coming and were trying to diversify the business by takeovers of other companies. When Lionel died they were concerned about the future of their supply of equipment from Daniels and could see that the future lay in plastics. As a result, they made an offer for the business. However, the managers at Daniels, who had been used only to growth, and a world where nothing went wrong, recommended to

174

the Daniels family refusal. The family, who wanted to retain the business for the next generation, agreed. In some ways they were right because they were on the edge of the next revolution in plastics, but the outcome was not to be as planned.

A line of Herbert injection machines installed at Kodak Ltd in Stevenage. The twenty machines were supplied by Herbert but made by Daniels; Edgewick and Herbert machines at the Herbert factory undergoing tests.

Lionel had been chair of T.H. & J. up until his death, with the rest of the Board comprising his wife, Eric (Frederic) Daniels, A. Johnson, F. Miller, H. Dauncey and P. Miller.

Eric did not play an active role in the running of T.H. & J. before Lionel's death; he was primarily concerned with Daniels (CAM) and had been for many years. Eric and Lionel had not worked well together from an early time so the fibre-board business had been made autonomous, a separate limited company but with a majority shareholding owned by T.H. & J. Other shareholders included Eric and Mr Clutterbuck, who was a director and the key figure in running the business.

The remaining board members had been with the company for many years. Records from 1938 show that Herbert Dauncey was the Works Manager. By this time he lived at No1 Clarence Villas, a property owned by T.H. & J. from 1926 that was awarded as part of the role. Percival Rodway had been an engineer before promotion to the position on the Board, and Arthur Johnson was the Chief Draftsman who lived at Innesfree, the bungalow owned by T.H. & J. that had been lived in by Lionel in his early days of marriage and went with the role. Frank Miller was the Accountant, who lived in Courtlands from around 1940. By 1956 Johnson, Miller, Dauncey and Rodway were all on the Board.

175

Percival Rodway, Herbert Dauncey, Arthur Johnson and Frank Miller.

With so much apparent wealth of knowledge and experience on the Board it was assumed by the shareholders that the business would not unduly suffer with the loss of Lionel. However, that was not to be the case.

On Lionel's death Eric took over as Chairman of the Board. Lord Dickinson was already Secretary, brought onto the Board by Lionel probably because of his financial contacts and knowledge of the operations of bigger companies. The plan had probably been to become a PLC because of the growing size of the company and because the legal limit of fifty shareholders for a private limited company had been reached.

Over the next few years, the turnover continued to grow, but production costs increased faster because of the inflation in wages and materials and poor organization within the company, making it difficult to service the debts that had been accrued in the building of the new facilities.

A major share re-organisation was carried out in 1959 and so that the number of shareholders could pass fifty, the company became a PLC but was not quoted. This facilitated a new class of shares, debentures, being issued raising an additional £300,000 of capital for the business; the downside was the 8% return that was to be paid annually. The capital was used in part to pay off the debts in building new workshops, with the remainder ploughed back into the company. This resulted in a dilution of the Daniels shareholding but provided more funds.

'New' building and assembly shop, 1967.

In 1962 there were new offices built on the site of the tool room and the business was still buying other engineering businesses, such as James Gordon & Co Ltd. The decision was taken to sell some of the properties: 2 Rose Place and Lynton Fieldside were sold.

In reality, Eric had little hands-on at T.H. & J. and was a figurehead, the business being run by Johnson and Miller. But Lionel had been instrumental in most of the major contract deals and so Mr Burgess-Short, the Senior Salesman became a Director by 1962.

After the offer from Alfred Herbert Ltd for Daniels was turned down it was felt that the relationship with them changed. Orders did not meet targets and in later years T.H. & J. had production issues and quality issues leading to late deliveries. Alfred Herbert used these issues as reason to sell fewer units. In reality they were struggling and had lost direction, details that were lost on the Daniels business and cause additional friction. The products were large moulding presses and not the type of unit that could be stocked, and although there was a good market for products, there was also increasing competition from abroad. T.H. & J. had aspirations to develop newer models, but Alfred Herbert could not commit the resource.

177

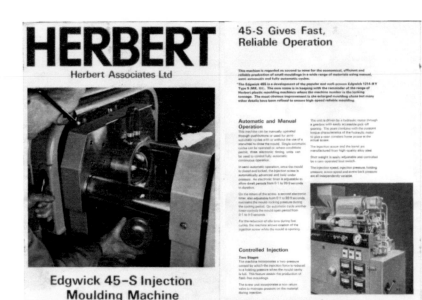

The brochure for an injection moulding machine made for Herbert by Daniels

T.H. & J. changed strategy and tried to sell more plastics equipment directly to customers, thus cutting out the 10% commission fee, but they did not have the marketing power that Herberts commanded. But Daniels probably did not realise the problems being experienced at Herberts as there was a decline in their business.

By 1963 Johnson, who was Managing Director of Daniels, together with Miller, continued to run the business. Burgess-Short and Eric were also on the Management Board but other staff members were only called upon when needed.

In 1963 the overdraft facility at Lloyds Bank was increased to £350,000. The business was not making the profits required to pay back for the investments in new plant that had been made and the business was struggling to keep up with the order book. In addition, the remaining shareholding in J. Clubley Armstrong (Danarm) Ltd was offered to T.H. & J. and additional funding was required. A total of £125,000 was paid for the Danarm business in January 1964.

The dilemma had been that T.H. & J. carried out much of the manufacturing of saws and didn't want to lose the output; however, the turnover of the business turned out to be much less than forecast: from an initial estimate of Dararm having 50% market share it transpired they had just 14%. In an attempt to cut costs, in 1964 the Danarm offices in London were closed and the business transferred to Slad Road in Stroud.

The manufacturing facilities were struggling: the Management Minutes talk of areas, such as the Plate Shop, being overloaded one year, only to be idle the following year. Key skilled employees who had been loyal to Lionel, such as Mr Cole and Mr Baker in the Sheet Metal Shop, left to go to competitors. The Board continued to re-organize departments, hoping to solve the problems: the Buying Department was moved away from the main offices.

Staff motivation suffered. 1963/4 saw the removal of staff perks as the business required more capital; workers saw the 25 Club stopped and both the foremen's and superintendents' Christmas parties stopped; help for private study books were stopped; the free Christmas turkeys for all staff members were also stopped. The "Cowley Conference", a brainstorming, team building and planning event for Management and staff had been held annually. The 1963 meeting, held locally to save costs at the Moor Court Hotel in Amberley, was the last. All purchases now had to be referred to the Board; in 1963 this included the purchase of a dictaphone and technical books, minor expenses taking up valuable management time. But the Directors still believed that they had sufficient funds for a new Directors' Dining Room to be built on the pretext of a facility suitable for visitors, and the Directors approved Diners Club Credit Cards for themselves, and Directors now travelled first class.

In 1964 Eric resigned as Chairman and Mr D. S. Robinson took over the role. He was brought in to turn the business around and brought a new approach, which included the cessation of prayers at the start of each meeting. However, he made little difference to the underlying business.

Also in 1964 there were still lots of building works on site: there were changes to the entrance to make it grander; there was a new Drawing Office built and new stores, all at significant expense. To help pay for the changes the Board sold the remaining housing stock – Fieldside in Rodborough Avenue, Greystone Lodge in Bath Road, Pretoria Villa, Lynton in Burdon Road, Stonehouse and Rose Villa.

By 1965 the Board had severe problems with delivery: in one month there was £58,000 on late delivery, and so a decision was made to investigate an additional plant. The Government had designated an area in South Wales as a development area. Traditional industries had closed and unemployment was high. As a result, grants were available to companies opening factories in the region. Government grants were on offer and a grant was seen by the Board as a way of obtaining more funding.

The first factory viewed turned out to be already sold, but another nearby in Dowlais near Newport was still available and was bought by Daniels. In reality it was little more than a shed in a field and a badly conceived plan. There were no local skilled engineers; the workers available were miners and foundry workers. In addition, significant training was required on the T.H. & J. product range, thus leading to a further drain on the limited skilled resources in Stroud. The site was fitted out by T.H. & J. as a sheet metal shop, paint shop and assembly plant, but in the first winter it was discovered there was no heating and the roof leaked, so production was lost until a new roof and heating systems were installed, an unexpected expense on a business already short of capital.

The plant continued to be a drain on the resources at Stroud for several years: it was impossible to channel a steady stream of work to the site; it was too far away and difficult to get to, and so some of the time the site was idle, and what work that was produced was poor. Parts were often missing from kits supplied from Stroud so a driver would have to make a special journey to the site to deliver. In reality, there was little enthusiasm amongst the workforce in Stroud for the experiment to work, taking their jobs, requiring their expertise and time when they had enough problems in their factory, and the project was doomed from the start.

Meanwhile Daniels (CAM) was doing well. In February 1962 it reported a new sales record and the trend was positive. It typically reported good profits and in 1966 reported £18,000 profit on a £220,000 turnover. This is where Eric spent most time and where most of his interests and allegiances lay, although it is generally accepted it was Mr Clutterbuck, the Manager, who was the driving force, and indeed earned a higher salary.

The next generation of Daniels were coming of age and, having served apprenticeships at other companies, joined T.H. & J. Daniels. John joined in 1958 having served an apprenticeship at Alfred Herberts. He worked on the management of the shop floor and was given tasks such as implementing Health and Safety policy, as new legislation was being introduced by the Government. Daniels had bought Hill & Enderby, a company based in Mousehole in Cornwall. The general engineering company was acquired to increase capacity and had skills in lathes and milling that were able to support the Daniels production facility, which was stretched. The local Manager was a Mr Williams, but John was assigned the role as Managing Director.

David had carried out his engineering apprenticeship at Fielding & Platt (Hydraulic Engineers) in Gloucester where he gained experience in every department.. With night studies and a one-day-a-week release, he had managed to obtain the equivalent of an Engineering degree and finished with an equivalent of an MIMechE. Following this, he went on to his two years' national service, and with this background the Air Force was pleased to give him the status of a Pilot Officer. He was posted to look after first-line servicing of the Chipmunks that the army pilots used for training. He was doing his two years' national service in the Air Force at Middle Wallop when the news came on that fateful day when his father died, and the company applied for his early release; so instead of being in the Force until November, he joined the firm in the middle of the summer 1958. Following this he joined the design team.

Of his early days, David writes:

'Initially I looked around the various works departments and then went to the Estimation Department in the Drawing Office. A fascinating place because as engineers, we had a reputation for producing 'anything wanted'. I had detail drawings of machines to give a manufacturing price for. Of course, loads of our own machines for injection moulding were upgraded and had to be priced. We did not stop at injection moulding. Our range of plastic machinery included:

(1) 'Vacuum Forming' for forming flat plastic sheets.

(2) 'Extruders' for forming tubes and pipes. Hydraulic presses had of course been our main product for years and we developed new models constantly. We also made metal die-casters both vertical and horizontal. We were up for special machinery and built a hydraulic track that was able to manipulate the Rover car engine block being passed down from position to position as the various machine processes took place.'

Daniels was always keen to embrace new ideas and it was whilst he was working here that he suggested injection moulding rubber, an idea that had not been tried before. The experienced engineers understood the problems in that it would set before the injection process could be carried out, but for some reason they allowed him to try. As predicted, it did set, but they tried adapting the machine to cool the mixture in a way to enable it to flow, and after a few weeks they had a solution that resulted in a machine to injection- mould rubber. The potential of the idea was huge, and David presented technical lectures around Europe extolling the new technology, but the ideas, which were ten years ahead of the competition, were not embraced by the management; there was no drive to sell the machines as the potential applications were not realised, and it was a time of frustration for him when he felt the need to do more. The company applied for patents but the Japanese had had similar thoughts and started to sell similar products. A while later, David became Managing Director of Pratt Daniels, a position he was to hold for the next few years, making it into a successful operation.

However, there were other positive activities. In 1964 Daniels went into partnership with The Parkson Industrial Equipment Company of Fort Lauderdale, America to create Daniels Parkson Ltd. The American company was wholly owned by The Parker Pen Company and the purpose of the new company was to develop and market a continuous high speed evaporating process for the food, latex, chemical and pharmaceutical industries. The move was had synergy with Daniels BBA, a company wholly owned by Daniels, which specialised in heat exchangers and process plant.

Brochure for Daniels Rubber Moulding Equipment showing applications from washers, grommets and bicycle pedals to hot water bottles and shoe treads; a Hydromold machine for rubber moulding.

Peter Daniels joined in 1964, having served an apprenticeship at another company, however, he did not have much chance to create any impact because by this stage the company was in chaos, and he was made redundant in the first wave of redundancies in 1965. Disenchanted with engineering, he left to set up another business.

It is likely that relations between Eric and the rest of the Board were difficult. An outsider to the business, Eric had been thrown into a position of Managing Director when others probably felt themselves more suited. He was comfortably off: as eldest son he had inherited from his father Frederick and his uncle John Stuart, who in turn had inherited from the previous generation. He had started working at Daniels CAM in 1929, had moved onto the board of T.H & J Daniels in 1937, became a Director of CAM in 1944 and Managing Director in the 1950's. He was made Chairman in 1965. Eric was single and in reality did not need to work. Family members recall how he would turn up for work mid-morning, then proceed to chat for hours, clearly lonely living on his own. At one time he had a share 'tip-off', and others were surprised that he had invested only a few pounds, but he had no desire to make money, just an interest in whether the 'tip-off' was correct. Eric could have invested more of his money in Daniels, but did not; maybe he was wiser than others gave him credit for. But this lack of support must have rankled with the Board.

David, who had by now joined the Board, could now see that things were not as they were supposed to be with the company. He had been Managing Director at Pratt Daniels, during which time it had been successful. The company

182

manufactured and installed dust collection plant using electrostatic precipitation and cyclones that collected the dust and fed it into large tanks. A major application at the time was the removal of dust from the exhaust chimneys in coal-fired power stations, such as the chimneys at Peterborough Power Station. There was not enough office space at the Daniels site, so the company had been based at Whitecroft from the 1950s. The company consisted of a team of mechanical engineers and draftsmen, project managers and sales staff. Manufacturing was carried out at the main site and installers and navvies were hired on a project basis for the installation tasks required. The company was an offshoot of an American company, based in New England, which was where the idea of using electrostatics had originated.

David now tried to rectify the situation with the main Board. He disagreed with some of the decisions being made, but his inexperience in politics resulted in an outcome that did not move the situation forward, and ultimately he chose to leave the company in 1965, but remained on the Board until 1969.

Meanwhile, orders for plastic moulding equipment were reasonable, but the designs were complex and the company was struggling to organize itself. The upheaval in industry nationally was causing problems in the procurement of parts, resulting in difficulties in controlling costs and requiring increased technical support. Industrial upheaval was causing additional problems in the traditional engineering businesses: large orders won for short-term delivery, requiring overtime, would be followed by periods without work, and profitability was affected. Projects in the development labs mushroomed out of control as more customers were requiring 'specials', and the new ideas within the industry created more opportunities for development, many of which required significant funding. This resulted in minimal focus on product re-engineering aimed at cost reduction to meet the competition from overseas. In addition, after the autocratic leadership of Lionel, the Management was weak and lacked focused guidance. It was said that it was Lionel's intention that each son would have his own company to run, and that was how it looked to be going, but the downside of this was that the brothers were taken off-site most of the time and were not involved in the daily management of the business, which was going badly.

The Board were desperately seeking ways to shore up the business financially, and one solution lay in the sales of the other businesses. In 1966 T.H. & J. Daniels had a controlling shareholding of 83.5% in Daniels CAM; there were eight other shareholders, including Robinson, Dauncey and Rodway, leaving Eric as only a minor shareholder and in no position to prevent a sale. The T.H. & J. Board instigated an investigation into the future of Daniels (CAM). The company accountants reported the options.

Melamine press and examples of melamine ware.

They stated that there were three options. First, that T.H. & J. could buy the remaining shareholding from the minor shareholders, but that there was an element of doubt over the long-term viability of the business to compete, because competition in the industry was likely to be keener. This was a strange argument, because there were only two competitors and a third of the output from CAM went to Loakes, a shoe insole manufacturer in Leicester. The business was earning good profits and there was no reason to assume it would change. It is likely that they formed their opinion on the market from discussion with Mr Clutterbuck.

Secondly, they could liquidate the company; they claimed that the book value of the company was £76,000; however, in a liquidation it was unlikely that this would be achieved. In addition, Clutterbuck had a service agreement with eight years to serve, which would cost £21,000 to terminate. The remaining return on a closure would therefore be £35,000.

The third option was a sale. They reported that, rather strangely, Loakes had said that if the business was sold, he would take his business to a competitor. This information was as stated to them by Mr Clutterbuck. In addition, any purchaser would be looking for a further injection of capital to replace equipment, an unknown amount at some future date, and so the accountants recommended against this solution.

Clutterbuck had offered to buy the business for £40,000, which interestingly is just slightly more than they predicted it would achieve by closure, so they recommended a sale for £40,000.

The Board took the decision to sell to Clutterbuck and Eric left the Board in December 1967. Somehow the Board had failed to see that he was acquiring a business for £40,000 that was returning £20,000 a year in profits, and he would be able to pay off a loan in just two years. In addition, by making Eric redundant he could save a further £3,000 a year in salaries if necessary. However press reports

184

indicated that Eric left to concentrate his efforts on Daniels CAM and indeed he was involved later with CAM's customers.

For the T.H. & J. Board, from a financial standpoint this was a mad decision to make. Businesses were returning around 8% on capital at the time; this would have obviated a trade sale in the region of £250,000. It is possible that this was done to spite Eric, but since they also had shares, they lost out, too. It must simply have been that they had no idea what they were doing and were badly advised, and we can only assume they ran the rest of the business as poorly.

Daniels Cam continues to this day in the same factory, manufacturing Sundeala board for a wide variety of applications.

Later, T.H. & J. cut Eric's pension. Eric, together with John, invested in the Stonehouse Paper & Bag Mills. John left T.H. & J. and went to run the business together with Mr Corrigan.

In 1970 Eric, aged sixty-two, was killed in a tragic car accident on the very day he was returning from a business meeting to apparently buy a share in Loakes. His 40% shareholding was a personal investment. As Chairman of CAM, then his investment in their biggest customer would have given him a greater say in the operation and his future.

What was strange was that Eric was travelling in a car with the company accountants as a passenger when he fell out and was killed. Nobody else was hurt. These accountants had advised against the visit and the deal, and were the same accountants that had advised T.H & J. that CAM should be sold to Clutterbuck. Eric may have indulged in a celebratory drink that resulted in his opening the door, but the accident happened on the Cirencester bypass, where the road joins from Bourton, and he would have been sober after several hours in the car. He was buried just 5 days after his death and no police investigation was instigated.

The cash injection proved valuable to Loakes. At the time, Leicester was the heart of the UK shoe manufacturing industry, but times were more difficult than was reflected in the books of the business. The injection maintained the business and, of course, helped to support CAM whilst the Daniels family suffered more losses.

It is difficult to imagine the burden felt by Helen, Lionel's wife. As the major shareholder, the responsibility for the business lay at her door, but she was no businesswoman but a Doctor of Medicine. Lionel had wanted the sons to enter the business and to each run a part of it. But without Lionel and without Eric, she will have felt quite alone. To see the decline of the business, with good staff leaving, will have broken her heart. When Peter was made redundant he had no redundancy pay, a young family to support and a qualification in a trade that was going through a deep recession, when there were no jobs.

185

Lionel had said that when he retired he wanted to run a restaurant and when David left the business he decided to do just that. He ran a garage business, following which he set up a restaurant.

Only John stayed in the Rodborough area; by the time he left he was seven years on his career ladder and saw an opportunity to acquire a personal stake in a local bag mill, where he worked for many years before a sad and untimely early death.

The Daniels had no continuity plan; they just believed that the business would continue. The Board Members who were not Daniels had grown up man and boy in T.H. & J.; they had been chosen by Daniels to fulfil an administrative role, a necessity in a modern company, and everything had been provided for them by the company, even their houses. They had led a closeted existence. For the first time they had go out into the real world and win business; they had to take charge of the factory and run it efficiently whilst motivating a highly skilled workforce, and keep it all in budget. Lionel had known every member of staff by name and knew what they were doing week by week. He knew every customer and personally visited sites regularly all over the world. He was a member of several technical institutions; he wrote technical papers, wrote reviews on other works for technical publications, attended a great many technical lectures and held technical meetings with other local engineering businesses. He was in tune with politics and knew MPs and other influential figures in Government and Commerce, and the business was missing him.

So in 1965 the board brought in consultants. The outcome was a savings programme that was focused on reducing labour, and so at the same time as Dowlais was being set up, there were redundancies at Stroud.

In 1967 T.H. & J. made a loss of £30,000 on a turnover of £1.5M. In May there were further redundancies including the gatekeeper, a loyal servant who had always said 'Good morning' to Lionel on his arrival before everyone else arrived. Dowlais was closed and fourteen staff made redundant. The Daniels family could not sustain any losses, the bank loans were high and the business had nothing left of value to sell.

In 1967, just nine years after Lionel died, the final Christmas party for the children was held.

In April 1968 the company received an offer for the business from Leeds Engineers Greenwood & Batley. The offer was again refused by the Daniels family and the shareholders, still believing the company could be saved and thus keeping it in tact for the workforce. In May 1968, after a Boardroom battle, Mr Robinson the Chairman of T.H & J Daniels at the time resigned and Dr. Helen Daniels took over as Chair. Just 8-weeks later a deal was brokered with Unochrome International for £844,000 for the 128 year old business, and in October the deal was completed for them to make machinery for the plastics, packaging, rubber and electronics industries. The name was changed to Daniels of Stroud and the Daniels family left the business.

It is interesting to note that under Helen's leadership, determined to save the business, the company recorded its highest- ever monthly sales of £400,000, of which £280,000 was from Alfred Herbert. The Martek mixer project in engineering that had been on-going for several years, and cost the company £41,613 in stock alone for potential sales of £200,000, was stopped: it could never have made money whilst engineering carried out eight new developments on the RV500 mixer. Danarm also reported improved business with sales of £46,000 a month to the Forestry Commission, and they started the manufacture of hedge-cutters and mowers. And the company returned to profit without relying on the sale of assets. Dr. Daniels had always believed that there were tasks suitable only for men, unyet she proved it wrong but discovered it too late!

Dr Daniels said ' It is rather sad to see the firm pass out of the family's hands, but we became a public company in 1961 and when you do that the family interests diminish considerably'.

Mr Owens of Unochrome became Chair and two other Directors from Unochrome joined the Board enabling the business some freedom to operate independently as it was now becoming profitable, and Helen now left. However, the company soon returned to loss.

Orders for the foundry were by now hard to win. Containers were made for Permutit Water Softeners in London, but there were no other large customers, so in 1969 the company bought Holmes, a foundry in Huddersfield, transferred the Permutit work to Holmes and closed the site at Stroud, making further staff redundant.

Later that year Mr Burgess-Short, the Sales Director, left the company. The company continued to trade through the 70s; Johnson remained on the board, his knowledge invaluable, but all the other members were new. Turnover was around £200,000 a month, but the company was blighted by problems with design faults and manufacturing faults in the presses. The biggest customer remained Herberts and factory output was dictated by Herberts' sales success. The company approached Herberts to see if they were interested in buying Daniels of Stroud, but they were having financial issues of their own.

Eventually John Brown, the great Industrial giant and long-time tool-maker, took over Unochrome, and the manufacturing facility dwindled so that only a small service section remained. The firm finally closed in 1986.

Chapter 28. Today

The site became an Industrial Estate, named Daniels, and today (2013) there are still around 100 people employed in a wide variety of businesses.

A business called Springfield Engineering was started by an ex-Daniels apprentice in Stonehouse, and took over the servicing and support work of Daniels when the business closed. The company re-located onto the Daniels site and carried on a general engineering business, competently taking over where Daniels left off. At one stage the company had over 100 staff, using all the same buildings built by the Daniels, and is still in occupation today, some thirty years later, with around fifty staff.

However, in 2012 the owners of the site received permission from the Council to knock down the buildings and build a supermarket. Government policy dictates that it is preferable to build on 'brown field' sites, and as a result, many engineering businesses have been closed throughout the country because the land is more valuable for other uses. In addition, the designated 'Industrial Heritage' area for the valley does not include the site but runs along its boundary, and as a result, there was no need for an enquiry, and indeed, there was not even a press notification. For a historic key site, in a prime location of some 3.4 ha, this may seem a little strange.

If you visit today, (2013) you will find Fern Cottage; Joseph's cottage, abandoned. Converted wholly to offices by T.H. & J. and the heart of the operation for almost 100 years, this is how it now remains. The original mill buildings are locked up and empty, and the first iron building built by Joseph on site, still sure and watertight, has clearly been used until recently, although it now lies empty.

Wander down through the site and one is forgiven for thinking that the whole site is abandoned, but clear a spy hole in the years of dirt through the small glass pane of one of the numerous metal casement windows of the main factories and you will find activity. Machines are still in operation. Entering through a door in the south side of the main factory, turn right and climb the steel steps up to a gallery that looks the whole length of the building, 1,000 feet, maybe more. Large presses and machines are running, machines that are fifteen feet tall look small in the vastness of the building, and there are many of them, mean and hungry for work.

Gantry cranes are located the length of the building, huge bulbous engines mounted on impressive looking steels that reach the width of the building, resting on wheels. The gallery is wide and useful with evidence of machines and activities, a railing for safety, and at one end is an entrance, now sadly bricked up, which would have given access to the next building and so on up the site to the offices. This is where my forefathers trod and viewed the frenetic activities in the factory; but it was not just a viewing platform: manufactured items could be lifted onto it by crane and wheeled through to the next factory, one level further up. This was the artery of the business bringing the life-blood from the heart, which was the foundry and the brains in the offices. It is easy to imagine how busy it was as staff hurried to and fro carrying drawings, instructions and parts, kits of bits issued to the shop floor for assembly of parts made in the foundry, maybe still warm from the flames that made them.

From the gallery on the other side was access to the toilets, now beaten, chipped and very 'Victorian', in their heyday a wonderful amenity for the staff, a well-appointed brick- built building with running water, a facility that befitted a generous employer. Further on was likely access to the next building, now blocked also.

Back outside, and a way can be found around the outside: an old sign indicates a reception past a series of temporary cabins. Another large warehouse, and entering through big doors into another part of the factory is a part busy with activity. There are smaller machines, although these are still large. Modern lathes clad in metal panels for safety, with electronic programmers that can take instructions directly from a computerised design system, stand where once, a hundred years previously, there were lathes controlled by man and driven by foot treadle. The machines are different, quicker, more accurate, more reliable, but the final results are the same: parts machined for use in bigger assemblies.

There are presses for pressing metal sheets into desired shapes and drills that can carry multiple bits, which can drill holes to within fractions of a centimetre – activities carried out by eye and with great skill by our forefathers: the accuracy was all-important, to within thousandths of an inch. The men of old, man and boy, learned the skills to achieve great accuracy on large and complex parts. If they got it wrong, then work would have to be started again with a loss of time and materials, and worst of all, reputation.

A warehouse in the old part of the site is full of abandoned equipment, but in the corner is a small hole in the wall through which is an underground reservoir and tunnels used for munitions storage, now full of files containing the history of Daniels of Stroud.

But there is still great skill and pride with today's men, here at work. They understand tolerances and materials; they live and breathe engineering; they understand the new computerised world of computer-aided manufacture, know its limitations and how to get the best from their tools, just as the men of past taught them. It is in their blood, as if an extension from the business heart and artery passes into their very being, providing them with unique talents for creativity. These are the men who have continued to make Britain 'Great' through into the modern day.

Despite the activity, there is an unerring gloom about the place, a melancholy; maybe the place is aware that its days are numbered. Another warehouse is full of old machines and equipment, stacked up the sides and strewn over the floor, each item having its own story to tell, not yet consigned to history and soon to be scrapped for its metal content. Strangely, the smell of oil lies still thick on the air, the smell of machines, a faint aroma of degreasant, swarf, and electrical ionisation, although the dust tells that it's lain here for a long time.

We've left the shop where the boilers were built, metal sheets drilled ready for the rivets, then formed into large cylindrical vessels before being hammered together, tops and bottoms added and riveted, or latterly, welded. And now we are in the foundry – not that it was always thus. As the factory spread through the years, so did the activities. The foundry was the pumping heart; it grew to absorb areas built to house the growing assembling and machining shops as they moved on into new, more modern factories, all interlinked, all sharing a common purpose. But it was in this vast warehouse, in the centre of the site, that giant piece parts were cast, bridges, wheels, engines and beams, and it is here that the large flat metal plates were made for turning into the boilers. In this warehouse, it is still now, but I can sense the activity; the heat from the foundry is trapped in the building and spreads easily from its location at the end.

We make our way now over a barrage of equipment that runs the building's length, in part physically climbing the pallets and using the sturdy machinery to hold onto to steady our path; our goal is a small hole in the wall on the far side of the warehouse. We pass into this innocuous cave, lit by a single light, to discover a sizable space that belies its outward appearance: a cave of some twenty-five feet in length, stuffed with archives of Daniels drawings, filing cabinet upon filing cabinet, lifetimes of work for men poring across drawing boards to produce finely detailed cross-sections of machines and mechanical assemblies – skilled men capable of such imaginative visualisation, so that, with only pencils and paper as the tools of their craft, they could lay down a blueprint for others to follow. This part of the site is little known, a secret bunker in the bowels of the buildings, located below the staff facilities area; many who spent a lifetime on the site will not have learned of its existence. It is where explosives were stored and history was made. We explore further: through bricked-up holes there are the water courses and wells that have supplied the site's clean, fresh water – water needed in the processes to form iron and steel, needed again for cooling machines to grind, cut and form.

Here we have discovered the underground water tanks that supply the sites water and the caves built to house the ammunitions deep under the site so that any German bombs would cause no devastating explosions. There are cages for security and you can imagine the explosives being moved in and out onto the manufacturing floor, this area is a hidden part of the site where few people would venture. In reality there were no bombs dropped over Stroud, only one German plane was reported to have flown up the valley and the factory was never identified as a bomb making factory by the Germans. There is clearly more, more tunnels and tanks, and another entrance, maybe buried explosives and traps in the event of a German invasion. What more is hidden away on this vast, sprawling site.

I am moved: this is my Heligan, my Tutankhamen, my history as much as any man, or woman, who ever worked on the site. To tread where great men toiled to make history, from the pin machines and gas generators to presses, bridges and plastic moulding, is a privilege. These were clever people!

With reluctance we leave the cave and move to the side of the buildings nearest the lower road. The building opens onto a platform about thirty feet above the road; from here, the horse-drawn carriages, laden with iron, would stop in the road below and goods winched onto the site, goods too heavy to pull up the steep inclines. It is 1900 and a large boiler is being moved towards the edge; there are six, maybe a dozen, workers pushing it on rollers, attaching the chains of the crane and inching it towards the precipice. They are working against the clock. It needs delivering, but this stage is critical: get it wrong and the boiler, maybe a few tons, will plunge down the cliff. This was how most large items were shipped from the factory, crane-load after crane-load of the most skilfully made products, a wealth of diversity and the engine house of the Industrial Revolution.

We make our way back up the site to the newer buildings, parts built in the '40s, '50s and extended in the '60s, more new parts in the '50s and '60s, continually evolving to meet the needs of the business. There are wider roadways, extended entrances and new warehouses. It's a veritable bombardment of information and it's as if we are on fast- forward, the years flashing past as we step forward in time up the hill, back into modern- day reality as we pass the latest buildings and approach the car park.

Soon the buildings will be silenced and likely felled, drawing a final veil over the site's engineering history – just another business from the Industrial Revolution that rose to greatness before a sad decline into oblivion, but the stories will go on through the people, and the skills and knowledge will not be lost; engineering will go on in the valleys, enthusiasm for the thrill of the science passed on 'through man to boy'.

Much of the information contained within this book is in the public domain, the Records Office and Museum. Thanks have to go to those who took the time and trouble to ensure that documents and photographs were safely deposited, and I somewhat feel that it's the positive enthusiasm towards the company that has ensured that so many memories have been kept by so many. It is impossible to tell the full account of all those employed, of the fun they will have had as well as the hard graft and long hours they toiled, but I hope this book paints a picture of a good and prosperous place to be throughout the 173 years 1840 to 2013.

And, as for the Daniels, most went their own way, although a nearby paper mills, bought by John Daniels, the eldest brother, to run as an autonomous business is still owned by some of the Daniels family and continues to trade. The Daniels family are now spread far and wide, although engineering still seems to run through the blood. In my generation, the seventh generation on from the start of the engineering business, all three boys, me included, have been involved in some form of technical engineering role. We look forward to discovering how the eighth generation fair in a world very different from the 19th and 20th centuries. My son is already following in his ancestors' footsteps and will shortly qualify as a Structural Engineer whilst my daughter has a career in Medical Science.

Sources

Thank-you to members of the Daniels family and other family relatives who have provided a wealth of information, memories and photographs. We are fortunate that Daniels photographed so much of the activity on-site and that so many photographs exist together with extensive records and a Family Bible.

Thank you also to Stroud Museum with whom the Daniels have a connection from its inception, to those who have passed on information and those on the Daniels site on Bath Road for their help.

Bodlean Library & Balliol College, Oxford
British Museum, India Office, London
Canadian Intellectual Property Office
Fakenham Museum of Gas
Gloucestershire Archives
Gloucester Citizen Newspaper
Gloucestershire Society of Industrial Archaeology
Herbert Museum & Archives, Coventry
Library and Museum of Freemasonry, London
National History Museum, London.
National Newspaper Archives, Colindale.
National Records Office, Kew.
Remembering Rodborough
Stroud Museum and Archives
Stroud News & Journal Newspaper
.

www.british-history.ac.uk
www.ancestry.com
www.stroudlocalhistorysociety.org.uk
www.rememberingrodborough.org.uk

Bibliography

David Dougan
The great gun-maker. The life of Lord Armstrong.
Sandhill Press 1991

John Griffiths
The third man. The life and times of William Murdoch.
Andre Deutsch Limited 1992

John Stuart Daniels.
The Woodchester Glass House. A record of the work of the
Hugenot Glass Workers. Published 1950

Leyla Maniera
Cristie's Century of Teddy Bears. Pavilion 2011.

L C A Knowles
Industrial and commercial revolutions in Great Britain during
the 19th Century. George Routledge 1941

Pauline Cockerill
Jungle toys rediscovered. Teddy Bear Times Aug 2005

Philip Parker
World History. Dorling Kindersley 2010

Roger Lloyd-Jones and M J Lewis.
Alfred Herbert and the British Machine Tool Industry.
Ashgate Publishing 2006

Rudyard Kipling
Plain Tales from the Hills. Oxfords Worlds Classics

S G H Loosley
Wycliffe College – The first hundred years.
Gomer Press 1982

Sidney Daniels
The case for electoral reform. Published 1938.

Victor Skip
The making of Victorian Birmingham Brewin Books 1996